Previous books by the author:

TWICE UPON A TIME, Moody Press
IN GOD'S HAND, Chalice Press
A FRESH WIND IN YOUR SAILS, West Bow Press
TO LOVE IN RETURN, West Bow Press
CLANGING HALYARDS, West Bow Press

Today Belongs To You

Donald D. McCall

WESTBOW
PRESS®
A DIVISION OF THOMAS NELSON
& ZONDERVAN

WestBow Press books may be ordered through booksellers or by contacting:

WestBow Press
A Division of Thomas Nelson & Zondervan
1663 Liberty Drive
Bloomington, IN 47403
www.westbowpress.com
844-714-3454

Because of the dynamic nature of the Internet, any web addresses or links contained in this book may have changed since publication and may no longer be valid. The views expressed in this work are solely those of the author and do not necessarily reflect the views of the publisher, and the publisher hereby disclaims any responsibility for them.

Any people depicted in stock imagery provided by Getty Images are models, and such images are being used for illustrative purposes only. Certain stock imagery © Getty Images.

[Scripture quotations are] from the New Revised Standard Version Bible, copyright © 1989 the Division of Christian Education of the National Council of the Churches of Christ in the United States of America. Used by permission. All rights reserved.

Scripture taken from the King James Version of the Bible.

ISBN: 978-1-6642-1134-6 (sc)
ISBN: 978-1-6642-1135-3 (hc)
ISBN: 978-1-6642-1133-9 (e)

Library of Congress Control Number: 2020921652

Print information available on the last page.

WestBow Press rev. date: 11/10/2020

Dedicated to:

Friends and Members
of
First Presbyterian Church
Rochester, Minnesota

Contents

Prologue

Most books are written to express an idea or to tell a story. Not this one. Its' origin harks back to a time in my own life when I was looking to God for some sign or inspiration to guide my future direction. It was not a time of despairing as much as it was a time spiritual searching. A quest that turned into a question. An inquiry that became an entreaty. I was beginning to sense that I was no longer preaching the Gospel as much as I was reaching out to solicit an audience. My ambition in early in life to motivate my congregation to a deeper faith and a more spiritual life. I felt that I had gradually morphed over the years into a I hadn't grown as quickly as they had. I sensed that I was preaching more to attract an audience than to share the gospel. I was never satisfied on Sunday if I didn't hear the scrambling of ushers setting up folding chairs for the overflowing crowd in the Sanctuary. I wanted them to have the same Sunday expectations that Theophilus had when Luke invited him to come to "know the truth" of all that he had heard about Jesus (Luke 1:4) To know the truth is more than to know the facts. The Greek language can translate 'know' as meaning 'encounter' and that's more than a handshake at the narthex door on Sunday morning. I wanted my congregation to know the truth about Jesus. I feared that I was sharing a handshake or a friendly word each week with them rather than the "dynamos" (dynamite) of the Gospel.

One Sunday as I finished preaching what I thought was a rather tepid sermon I closed with a prayer and then turned in the pulpit and slowly descended a few narrow steps until I reached the tiled chancel floor. As I walked back to my chair, I said to myself, "That's not the sermon I should have preached. It's not even the one that I wanted to preach." But it was one that I knew would be a sermon that the congregation would enjoy. My thoughts reminded me of an old story that my Homiletics professor at Princeton told me years ago: The Rev. John Bunyan, the author of <u>Pilgrim's Progress,</u> one Sunday walked to the church front door after worship and greeted one of his departing Elders who said to Rev. Bunyan while shaking his hand, "I just want to be the first to tell you, that was a great sermon that you preached today." Rev. Bunyan responded, "Ah, you're too late! The Devil already told me that as I stepped down from the pulpit."

That experience led me to a new time of introspection, so I set apart my first waking hour every morning to read the Scriptures and to contemplate the direction my life needed to take. After some months of this daily practice, I realized I also needed to write down what I was learning. It was a form of what we call journaling where with constant and incessant reading of scriptures, we come to emulate what they say and to discover new directions for our own lives.

As the months passed, I realized that my journaling habits could be shared with others who were probably experiencing the same dilemma of searching for meaning in their lives. So I gathered up some of my morning devotions and with the encouragement of local businesses that wanted to sponsor wider distribution of my thoughts, and sold them to the local NBC television station. They were aired at 7:29 for 30 seconds every morning, right before the Today Show. They were 30 second motivational spots. Every weekday I would appear on the screen, wearing the same suit, same tie and same smile to help viewers get their days started with a positive thought. These spots were broadcast throughout Southern Minnesota. They became a success beyond what I had imagined. Soon, I became better known as a motivational speaker than as a Presbyterian minister. I was amazed at the responses that TV program produced:

> One day a lady stopped me downtown and said, "I was getting dressed this morning and put on an old dress I wear all too often and then I heard your TV show and went back into the bedroom and put on a new dress I had just purchased and wore it to work. I had a wonderful day! Thank you so much!"
>
> On another occasion I was in Winona, MN. for a breakfast meeting and it lasted longer than expected so I stayed for lunch at the restaurant. After lunch I took my bill to the cashier and wrote her a check. As I handed her my check I asked if she needed identification. She looked up at me smiled and with a wink she said, "No...today belongs to you!"

Now some of those TV vignettes are being presented to you in book form, bringing them to life again for a second time. They are all taken from the teleprompter I used every day and in the same format that I used. My hope is that they will serve to inspire you and that you will enjoy them.

An Interjection

On the following pages I have put on paper some of the 30 second 'Inspirational Vignettes' reproduced exactly as they appeared on the teleprompter that I used to broadcast them every morning at 7:30. The goal of my daily broadcasts was to give the listener an uplifting moment as they began their day.

My show came on at the 7:30 a.m. news and weather break on the NBC's Today Show. Consequently, this book is entitled "Today Belongs To You" which was my TV sign off "bon mot" at the end of every vignette.

Furthermore, I have interjected a few sketches in between these commercial vignettes that I was recording each week. They were created for me by my daughter Karen. When she was a senior in high school she traveled with me to England and France and when we returned home she gave me a framed collection of her sketches of that trip which I now have above my desk on my study wall....I have waited a long time to display this new collection. I thank her for this collaboration.

In all my other books I have used photographs for illustrations of what I wanted to depict. Now I have these sketches that I will frame and hang at the left side of my desk and I'm sure you will understand why I now call this my favorite book!

These sketches represent some of the many trips that I have made through the years and which consequently have become a part of my thinking in what Jesus called his desert time. Jesus made many trips alone into the desert and wilderness places and I have found His practice to be a good model for my life and now for this book. I hope you enjoy it.

A Few of my Favorite Vignettes

A Vignette is a short descriptive paragraph that focuses on one moment or character or an idea that evokes a meaningful response. A Vignette stands alone and doesn't need to be connected to other stories or novels.

My tenure at First Presbyterian Church 40 years ago now rests in my mind as the memory of hundreds of thousands of wonderful memories. I have included a few of them in this volume as well as the vignettes that I created for my morning motivational TV show.

Let me share but one of the number of vignettes that I remember from my Rochester days:

At one of our monthly Session (Church Board) meetings we were all aware of the fact that one of our Elders was not present. We all knew that he had been hospitalized with a serious condition. That realization loomed over us like a dark cloud throughout the meeting. As the meeting was concluding I suggested that we adjourn to go to the hospital to allow the absentee member to share with us in the closing prayer and benediction. The group's response was unanimous and instantaneous. So off we went across the Mayo Clinic campus to the hospital. Seeing that we were such a large crowd we avoided the elevator and walked up two flights of stairs and then down the hall to our friend's room. His look of surprise and consequent smile at acknowledgement of our presence was a moment that none of us will ever forget. I offered a prayer and we all shared in the benediction:

"The Lord bless you and keep you; the Lord make his face to shine upon you, and be gracious unto you, the Lord lift up his countenance upon you and give you peace." (Numbers 6:24-26 NRSV) Amen

As we walked back to the church parking lot, I realized that I had for the first time in my life truly experienced the meaning of Jesus' words: "Where two or three are gathered in my name, I am there with them." (Matt. 18:20) We all had experienced His presence and our lives had been touched by Him.

Such was life at First Church and thus I hope you will enjoy some of my favorite vignettes which I have collected here for you and the unwritten texts which sparked the inspiration to write them.

Good Morning:

If Christopher Columbus would have turned back before discovering
America, no one would ever have blamed him. But then again,
no one would ever have remembered him either!
  Success belongs to those who persevere.
  <u>Today belongs to you</u> ... Persevere ... and make today count!

Good Morning:

If a carpenter spoils a piece of wood that he is working on, he
can throw it aside and take another piece in its place.
  But a parent cannot do that with a child,
  Nor a teacher with a student,
  Nor a friend with a friend.
  <u>Today belongs to you</u> ... share it with a friend.

Good Morning:

Although companionship is necessary for life, I do love being alone ...
to take time to reflect on life ... to examine its sense of direction.
For solitude is still the indispensable ingredient that inspires
the creative, productive mind.
  <u>Today belongs to you</u> ... Use some time of it to be alone.

Good Morning:

I like the imaginative dreams of the future more than the ancient history
Of the past. Yet what lies behind us and what lies before us are
Insignificant compared to what lies within us.
<u>Today belongs to you</u> … use it to bring forth the best that is
within you.

Good Morning:

Imitation is not, as one might think, a form of flattery. It is
Instead a visible expression of a lack of imagination. To imitate
Others is evidence of a loss of confidence in your own sense of
identity.
<u>Today belongs to you</u> … be yourself … be yourself!

Good Morning:

You can't plow a field by turning it over in your mind. Nor can you
accomplish any worthwhile task without taking that first step.
The secret of success, of getting ahead in life, lies in getting started.
<u>Today belongs to you</u> … use it to take that first step in
fulfilling your dreams.

Good Morning:

Socrates, the Greek philosopher, advised, "Know thyself." Modern philosophy suggests, "Be yourself." But the advice I like best is, "Don't be afraid to laugh at yourself."
<u>Today belongs to you</u> … and even if you are by yourself, don't
be afraid
To laugh at yourself.

Good Morning:

To build soundly for the future you have to think constructively in the present. Only by the addition of some positive ideas today can tomorrow's dreams ever come true.
<u>Today belongs to you</u> …Use it to nail down a new idea or two
to make tomorrow's dreams come
true.

Good Morning:

Beauty is not in what we see, but in how we see what we see. Therefore, to find that which is beautiful in the world you need only to look into your own heart … for it is the heart that interprets what the eye sees.
<u>Today belongs to you</u> … to make it a beautiful day, keep at
least one eye open to what your heart
perceives.

Good Morning:

Of all the gifts that we can five to one another in this world,
none is more precious than the gift of time, especially the time
we spend with one another. For time is the real measure in this
world of what we most truly treasure.

<u>Today belongs to you</u> … share some time today with those
whom you love.

Good Morning:

Sometimes it's easier to love the whole world than it is
to love your neighbor:
    And though "Living with the saints in heaven may be bliss and
    glory,
    living with your neighbors on earth is often another story!"
Showing a little kindness to your neighbor is often better than an
unexpressed world of love for all humankind.

<u>Today belongs to you</u> … share a little kindness.

Good Morning:

It's not what you own, but what you share that makes you rich.
The true joy of life is not found in what you possess but in
how you share what you have with others.
It's through sharing in life that your own life is enriched.

<u>Today belongs to you</u> … use it to share something of your life
with others.

Good Morning:

On this Labor Day let me express my concern for your personal
Safety as you travel to enjoy the holiday with family and friends.
Please! Drive as if you own the car and
Not as if you own the highway!
    <u>Today belongs to you.</u> … make it a safe day for yourself and others.

Good Morning:

The two things we can give our children are "roots" linking
them to the past, and "wings" to free them for the future.
Remember, that giving children the wings to soar on their own
is just as important as giving them roots, which in time
will be outgrown.
    <u>Today belongs to you</u> … Use some of it to nourish your
                                  children's roots before they fly off on
                                  their own.

Good morning:

The secret of success is not in getting ahead of others as much as
it is in helping others to fulfill their goals.
For your success in life is not only in living up to your potential,
but also in helping others live up to theirs.
    <u>Today belongs to you</u> … Remember: no one ever gets to the top
                                  By putting other people down.

Good Morning:

The secret of being a friend lies not in getting someone to like you
But in helping others to like themselves. Perfect friendship is knowing
And loving someone enough to bring out the best that is in that
person.

> <u>Today belongs to you</u> ... use it to be that best friend to someone.

Good Morning:

The person who has never made a mistake has never made anything!
The truth is that success often comes only after repeated failures.
The only real mistake you can make in life is to fear failure so much
that you give up trying.

> <u>Today belongs to you</u> ... use even today's mistakes to your future
> advantage.

Good Morning:

A life that is worth living is a life that is worth giving ...
worth being spent for others. The very essence of life lies in
being willing to risk it ... to spend it for something greater than
yourself.
It's still true that it is better to burn out than to rust out!

> <u>Today belongs to you</u> ...risk some of it for someone else.

Sleeping on the Shore of The Sea of Galilee

I rolled out my sleeping bag and camped on the beach at the Sea of Galilee near Capernaum and spent one of the most peaceful nights of my life. The stars were out rivaling one another to gain my attention until my eyes closed reluctantly to allow me a good night's rest.

Listening to the water gently lapping up to the shoreline in metronomic rhythm lulled me to sleep quickly as my mind drifted into the dreamland that the disciples probably shared on nights such as this in their travels with Jesus

Good Morning:

Some people pursue happiness wherever they go.
Other people create happiness wherever they are.
    For happiness isn't something out there
    Happiness is within you to share.
<u>Today belongs to you</u>…You don't have to pursue
                 What's already in you !

Good Morning:

Sometimes…desiring the impossible makes you work that much
    harder doing the probable … and keeps you from being
    satisfied with the mediocre…yet continually challenging
    to rise above yourself.
<u>Today belongs to you</u>…stretch yourself to the limit for success is
              saved for those who win it!

Good Morning:

Normally in life we are taught the virtue of giving
But the fact is that we often get back in life more than what we have
given.
    If we give friendship, we get back friendship
    If we give kindness, we get back kindness
    If we give love, we get back love…
<u>Today belongs to you</u>…..Don't be afraid to give your best away
             For it often comes back in some
             unexpected way.

Good Morning:

If you treat someone as if they were what they ought to be
then you help them become what they really want to be.
    For as flowers bloom best by the light of the sun
    So we bloom best when we're encouraged by someone
And though Today belongs to you, act as if it belongs to them
too !

Good Morning:

In a time when everyone is seeking someone else to emulate
    to be the pattern and model for their own lives,
Don't be afraid to be the person that others admire
For we all have qualities worthy of public adulation...

Today belongs to you . Don't be afraid to parade your good
                      qualities in public view.

Good Morning:

In this day and age of fast foods and microwave cooking is hard
to remember that sometimes its better to be patient than to be
insistent ...
better to be wiser than intolerant.
For everything in life doesn't have to be done right now.

Today belongs to you ....but then...tomorrow does too!

Good Morning:

Though haste makes waste, I know that is also true
that you don't have forever to decide what you want to do.
Sometimes when you sit down to count the cost
Some of life's best opportunities are lost !

Today belongs to you If you sit and think about it too long
                    The chance of a lifetime may forever be gone.

Good Morning:

A mind that is being used is also a mind that is being changed
And those who never change their minds are probably those who
never use them
    Those who hold that conformity is everything
    Are those who rarely think about anything.

Today belongs to you… do what you have a mind to do !

Good Morning:

Our hopes in life are often vague and rather distant
Whereas our fears are often precise and with us every instant;
    So the secret is to focus on what you hope and dream
    And to not let your fears intervene.

Today belongs to you… Don't let the fears that you feel
                    Keep your dreams from becoming real.

Good Morning:

Happiness is knowing you're going to win even before you dare to begin;
To know you're going to succeed, even before you dare to proceed.
Life's happiest moments are often moments of challenge,
Like salmon swimming upstream, if you know what I mean.

Today belongs to you and making it count is not so much a matter
                            of chance
                            As it is a matter of demonstrating your
                            perseverance

Good Morning:

Springtime is both rain and sun
Streams that glisten as they ripple and run,
Delicate leaves on new budding trees
And a mist on the daisies as they sway in the breeze.

Today belongs to you….Let the awakening of spring impart
                            The awakening of new hope in your heart

Good Morning:

Success in life lies in the power to believe
That you can achieve anything that your mind can conceive;
But that power lies in your own confidence and self-esteem`````````
In believing that you will fulfill your very hope and dream.

Today belongs to you…follow every dream that you'be ever
wanted to.

Good Morning:

With all the demands for your time for the week ahead
And with all the pressures of life that surround you
Take some time today to pamper yourself
And to treat yourself as you wish others would…

For Today Belongs to you and loving others begins with loving yourself.

Good Morning:

Going the extra mile is often considered to be an act of kindness.
And it's that kindness that often wins someone else's heart;
Now if walking the extra mile can do all of that
Can you imagine what would happen if you'd run!

Today Belongs To You …. Run with it

Good Morning:

Sometimes making decisions can be one of life's most difficult tasks
And yet knowing that not to decide is in its own way to decide
We come to realize that in not making those life decisions
We are foregoing the opportunity to determine our own destiny.

Today Belongs to You and only you can determine what you want to do.

Good Morning:

Sometimes we are so vain as we look at ourselves
That we forget how to look at ourselves in a lighter vein
    and we miss the chance to laugh at ourselves.
In not learning how to laugh at ourselves,
    we miss the chance to enjoy ourselves.

Today Belongs To You ... Learn to laugh at some of the silly
                    things you do.

Good Morning:

Sometimes a change of routine, a change of scene gives a different
perspective on life and also changes our view of life. Just as the
view from the top of the hill is different from that of the valley, so
elevating your mental attitude can change your work day attitude.

Today Belongs to You... Enjoy it from a hill top point of view.

Good Morning:

Joy in life comes not so much from what you own....what you
possess but rather from knowing what possesses you to be the person
that that you are. For its more important to know who you are than
to know what you own.

Today Belongs to You...Do you know what possess you?

A Side Trip to Sidon

When I was a boy my favorite beach in all the Holy Land was the beach located at Sidon. Its' sandy shore had what felt like the nap of a Persian rug and it's sheltering causeway gave it the calm swimming area of private lagoon. Locally it was called 'Jonah's Beach' because it was reputed to be the beach where Jonah was spewed out by a whale on to the land and I confess it always gave me the woolies to swim there, but I loved it. I can easily understand why Jesus took time for a side trip to Sidon with his disciples.

Now at midlife, as I was once again taking a side trip to visit my childhood's favorite beach I was reminded that what I remembered of those early years of my life wasn't so much about the Jonah story as it was about the truth that like Jonah, God also has purpose for my life. "I have a plan for you…to give you a future with hope." (Jer. 29:11-13 NRSV). I realized that I needed to be reminded that like Jonah I couldn't run away from my destiny.

I left feeling refreshed and renewed…just as in my childhood days after a brisk morning swim!

Good Morning:

Nothing in life is to be feared … it is only to be understood.
For it is in understanding … in knowing … that fear is destroyed
and you are able to do what you once thought was fearsome and
Impossible.
    <u>Today belongs to you</u> … use it to conquer your fears by doing the
Very thing you fear to do.

Good Morning:

Time is a gift that we all receive equally.
It's yours to use or to lose.
But life's value does not depend
so much upon the time we spend
as it does upon how we spend the time we choose.
    <u>Today belongs to you</u> … spend it as if it were your most valuable
possession.

Good Morning:

We often blame others for what happens to us in life
and what becomes of us.
But the important thing in life is not what becomes of you
but what you become, and you can control that.
    <u>Today belongs to you</u> … take control of it before it controls you.

Good Morning:

The long range plans you make for the future do not deal with decisions you'll make in the future, but with the future of the decisions you are making today. Your future happiness and success depend upon the decisions you make today.

   Today belongs to you … but live today with at least next week in mind.

Good Morning:

A friend is someone who not only adores you with the heart
but also who admires you with the mind.
For true friendship seeks not adoration alone but also that
admiration which inspires us to become greater than we are.

   Today belongs to you … use it to admire someone you adore.

Good Morning:

When we try to impress other people we often only suppress the possibility of their coming to know us as we really are.
For to know someone in the truest sense of the word means to be as open with them as you want them to be with you.

   Today belongs to you … so suppress that hidden urge to impress others.

Good Morning:

Finding fault is the only thing in the world you'll ever find
for which no reward is offered.
Yet, all too often we find fault with others … not in order to
change them … as much as to prove to ourselves that we are
exempt from their faults.
　　Today belongs to you … use it not to find fault, but to find
　　　　　　　　　　　　　pleasure in others.

Good Morning:

As the week begins … remember that the secret of success lies not in
what we begin … but in what we finish. The ability to preservers …
to follow through … is still the critical characteristic you need in life
to get from where you are to where you want to be!
　　Today belongs to you … follow through in whatever you do.

Good Morning:

Unless you go beyond yourself, you cannot find yourself. Self-knowledge
comes not so much from digging into one's soul as it does from one's
willingness to open up to others. For in sharing ourselves we discover
ourselves.
　　Today belongs to you … take time to share something of yourself
　　　　　　　　　　　　　with someone else.

Good Morning:

Life's greatest pleasures often lie in those unexpected surprises … those rare moments when we are taken off guard … and our hidden feelings of joy and love are instinctively expressed.

Today belongs to you … cherish its surprises as life's perfect prizes.

Good Morning:

Success in life often lies not so much in the future as it does in the present. For life's fulfillment lies not in what we might be as much as in what already is … in the use of what you already have, within arm's reach.

Today belongs to you … reach out and grab it!

Good Morning:

The old adage that "if a thing is worth doing at all, it's worth doing well" could rightly be changed to "if a thing is worth doing, it's worth doing even if done badly." For even if what we do doesn't produce excellence, it still gives one the satisfaction of a sense of achievement and accomplishment.

Today belongs to you … if you feel it's worth doing … do it!

Good Morning:

Nothing promotes productivity as much as praise.
Nothing promotes creativity as much as appreciation.
    The productive, creative person is one that is often
    surrounded by praise and appreciation.
    <u>Today belongs to you</u> ... surround someone with praise and
                        appreciation.

Good Morning:

Life is often hills and valleys
and though we sometimes have to walk through the valleys
life's highest and noblest moments and those we spend upon the hill
where our view of life is expanded
and our hearts and minds are expanded too.
    <u>Today belongs to you</u> ... save some time for the hill.

Good Morning:

Criticizing others is often a self-disclosure of one's own faults.
For when you point the finger of criticism at others ... remember
that you are pointing your other three fingers at yourself!
For what we dislike most in others is often what we fear in ourselves!
    <u>Today belongs to you</u> ... don't waste the best in you by
                    criticizing the worst in others.

Good Morning:

You only grow old in life when you stop dreaming …
when you close your mind to the possibilities of life yet before you.
To be young at heart is to always have an open mind,
always seeking to discover something new in life … in others …
and in yourself.

> Today belongs to you … take time to open your mind to
> something new.

Good Morning:

We feel fulfilled in life, not when we compete with one another
but only when we complete one another.
For to make another person's life full and complete
is also to be fulfilled oneself.

> Today belongs to you … fulfill ourself by giving yourself to others.

Good Morning:

A small investment in kindness can pay a big dividend
in someone else's life. It's through little acts of thoughtfulness
and unexpected small favors that we enrich our relationships
with one another.

> Today belongs to you … showing interest in others is a
> dividend to you.

A High Himalayan Hermitage

I was sitting here, cross-legged high in the Himalaya Mountains listening to a Sadhu (wise teacher) at an Ashram (study center) on Mount Kadernath, when in the course of his talk an ant crawled up my leg to my kneecap. Without thinking I reached down and with the back of my hand I swatted the ant off into ant eternity. The Sadhu, noticing what I had done, stopped his lecture ... looked at me and said, "Why did you do that? The ant wasn't bothering you." I was lost for a response. We do so many things instinctively. The Sadhu went on to talk about how often we hurt others without thinking about what we are doing or saying. Then he reminded us of the words of the Prophet Isaiah, "They shall not hurt nor destroy on all my Holy Mountain." (Isaiah 11:9 NRSV). The Sadhu went on to talk about being mindful and kind in the way we live together, the way we treat one another … and especially in the way we speak to one another.

It was a memorable mountain top experience for me.

Good Morning:

Time is one of life's greatest gifts to treasure
And one that we all receive in equal measure;
So, learn to use time before it uses you,
Take time for yourself before each day is through

Today Belongs to You... every hour and minute is waiting for you
to do something in it.

Good Morning:

It's often in adversity that confidence meets its ultimate test
And in those moments your confidence is simultaneously
strengthened and your external stress is diminished.
Problem solving often comes when we know we have the
confidence to solve our problems.

Today Belongs To You ... Give it your best as you face each daily test.

Good Morning:

Like lilacs which bloom only once in the springtime
So our lives are brief and soon they are gone...
But like lilacs whose fragrance lingers long after they've passed
So life's memories linger and continue to last.

Today Belongs To You: Let today's memories linger with you.

Good Morning:

Just as bread needs to be kneaded and shaped to refine its texture before it rises…so we need to learn that setbacks and disappointments are often but necessary steps towards shaping us for our future rise to success.

Today Belongs To You…and success does too.

Good Morning:

As summer comes and schedules change, we have the chance to get out of our winter ruts and seek unexplored avenues that lead to new challenges in life. Sometimes we need to be forced away from the old and familiar before we are willing to explore something different in life.

Today Belongs To You and it's your opportunity to try something new.

Good Morning:

Sometimes when a whole day seems to be spoiled when plans are suddenly changed we need to remember that it only takes one golden minute to make any day the happiest day of your life.

    For life is lived not in days and hours
    But in those moments that are eternally ours !

Today Belongs To You… Look for that golden minute that carries
               a whole day's happiness in it.

Good Morning:

Like small boats that follow in the wake of larger ships
We sometimes for safety's sake follow in the footsteps of our heroes;
But just as a small boat can be capsized by the wake of a larger one
So in life we can find ourselves so overwhelmed by the accomplishments
of others that we don't dare to venture out on our own.

Today Belongs To You... Set your own course....chart your own seas;
Do what you want to do...and be who
you want to be

Good Morning:

Summer vacation, though normally thought of as a time to get away
from it all, is also a good time to get it all together. A time to take
stock of yourself....a time to re-examine where you have been and
where you are going.

Today Belongs To You... don't let it pass without trying to do something
different, or to learn something new.

Good Morning:

Public opinion is not a law or a rule that needs to be obeyed,
It's only an opinion.
And confidence in life comes not from following public opinion as
much from learning to live in peace with your self....even if your
opinions are different than others.
For every opinion at its inception is minority point of view.

Today Belongs To You and your own opinion, if expressed,
may become the opinion of others too.

Good Morning:

Sometimes as we begin the day looking out the window to check the weather we allow the weather to determine our outlook for the day. For the brightness of the day is not dependent upon the sun as much as it is dependent upon how you feel about something or someone.

Today Belongs To You … Enjoy it, come rain or come shine!

Good Morning:

Happiness in life comes not in seeking pleasure for yourself but rather
    in seeking perfection in what we do.
Happiness lies not in seeking the things that we desire
    as much as in seeking life's highest goals to which we can aspire!

Today Belongs To You Let that be your highest guiding star.

Good Morning:

So often in life…it's something minor…something trivial
That destroys gatherings that should enjoyable and convivial;
    Usually it's a thoughtless word or an inconsiderate act.
But life is really more than what happens to you
It's really more about how you choose to react to what happens to you.

Today Belongs To You… don't let the little things get you down.

Good Morning:

Sometimes affirming someone else's presence through a glance
or by a touch is more meaningful than the formal acknowledgements
and greetings that we more commonly use.
For our formal greetings too often become formidable
Whereas our casual contacts tend to be more personable.

Today Belongs To You .. a wink is often appreciated more than
you think!

Good Morning:

Change is often painful because it means letting go of something
in ourselves.
It means risking what we have for what we want
It means risking who we are for who we want to be:

Today Belongs To You ... sometimes the cost of continuing to grow
is the need to risk letting some things go.

Good Morning:

It's true that you can't give away what you don't have or own.
You can't give away happiness if you're not happy
You can't give away peace if you're not at peace
You can't give away Love if you're not loving.

Today Belongs To You as does peace, happiness and love
try to give away at least one of the above.

Good Morning:

When you are worrying you are living in the future tense
When you are angry you are living in the past tense,
What we need to learn is how to live in the present tense
Not imprisoned by the past, nor afraid of the future.

Today Belongs To You ... live it in the present tense!

Good Morning

Balancing your budget today is hectic enough
Maintaining a balanced diet is equally tough;
But neither a balanced budget nor a balanced diet are adequate
enough to keep your life in balance.
It is that equilibrium we need in order to succeed.

Today Belongs To You ... balance your life with work and pleasure
                        bur not necessarily in equal measure

Good Morning:

If you don't enjoy yourself, you surely won't be able to enjoy other people
If you don't enjoy being alone, you won't enjoy doing things with others
For how you feel about yourself is ultimately how you will feel about
others.

Today Belongs To You ... keep some free time to enjoy your own
                        company!

With the Ruins of Phillipi at my feet

Often in life it's the little things that we encounter that make the greatest impact in our lives.

Philippians is one of the smallest books in the New Testament but in its pages I came across one of the greatest lessons in that we can learn in life.

The ancient village of Krenides, known for its gold mines, was conquered by Philip II of Macedon in 356 BC and after the discovery of new gold mines nearby, Philip renamed the city 'Philippi' to honor and memorialize himself and to let the world know of his ambitious plans to conquer the world. While I was walking about in the ruins of Philippi I was reminded of my favorite text from Paul's letter in the New Testament where he admonishes us *"Do nothing from selfish ambition."* (Philippians.2:3 NRSV). It was a never to be forgotten moment to be saved in my memory.

It's just one sentence in a brief book but as I stood at this spot and looked at the toppled ruins of an ancient city it reminded me that "selfish ambition" also has the power to topple and destroy my life and leave all my future hopes and dreams lying in ruin at my own feet.

I vowed there and then to live my life altruistically, not selfishly.

Good Morning:

The worst thing about people who give you advice
    Is that you know that they probably need it more than you do;
And since there is no way to tell good advice from bad advice,
    You might as well learn to think for yourself.

<u>Today belongs to you</u> …and to thine own self be true !

Good Morning;

Contrary to popular opinion it is not power that corrupts
But the fear of losing power, or of not knowing how to use the power
you have.

<u>Today belongs to you</u> …use what power you have for the common good.

Good Morning:

Fault finding in others has always intrigued me,
Inasmuch as there is no reward offered for all the faults you find in
them;
    And after all, the faults we find in others are really
    the faults we try to hide within ourselves.

<u>Today belongs to you</u> … Try to be generous to a fault.

Good Morning:

Sometimes the most beautiful part of the day is the remembrance
of the day before.
A reviewed vision, a memory of the past....
It is the memory of the past that gives us hope for the future.

<u>Today belongs to you...</u> Enjoy it to the point that it may be
                        Tomorrow's happiest memory.

Good Morning:

Sometimes when you feel that you are at the end of your rope
When you feel almost ready to give up all hope;
Tie a knot at the end of the rope and hang on a little longer.
For endurance is often the key to success, the difference between
winning and losing.

<u>Today belongs to you...</u> So hang in there until your dreams do
                        come true.

Good Morning:

The truth is that you can't build yourself up by tearing others down,
Nor can you make yourself taller by stepping on someone else's toes;
    We grow in life by making friends...not foes
    By what we accept...not what we oppose.

<u>Today belongs to you....</u> Believe me, that's how life goes !

Good Morning:

It's alright to pin a flower on someone's lapel
    As a gesture of love or affection,
But it's not alright to pin a label on anyone
For labels are often symbols of rejection.

<u>Today belongs to you…</u> and you'll discover as you get older, that a
                    flower on a lapel is better than a chip on
                    your shoulder.

Good Morning:

To speak the truth is an admirable quality of life.
It's a quality that sets you free from the complications of telling lies.
The danger is that we sometimes mistake 'opinions' for truth
And those opinions make you a prisoner of your own prejudices.

<u>Today belongs to you </u>remember that 'truth' is the key to setting
                    you free.

Good Morning:

It's more important in life to make friends than it is to
make money. It's just as important to spend as much time with
a friend as you spend making money.
For true friends maintain their value through recessions,
despite depression.
    <u>Today belongs to you</u> … Renew your interest in a friend.

Good Morning:

Leadership is not in demanding others to follow you, as much
as it is in challenging others to accompany you … to share life with
you as together you move from where you are to where
you want to be.

> Today belongs to you … be a leader by challenging others
> to accompany you as you follow your
> dreams.

Good Morning:

The most expensive gift that we can give to others in our time …
our sharing of ourselves with others.
For your personal presence is more valuable than all the presents that
gold or silver can buy.

> Today belongs to you … let your personal presence be your
> gift to others today.

Good Morning:

People are not to be valued because of what they possess
but rather for who they are.
For to cultivate friendships because of what others possess
is to secretly desire those possessions yourself.

> Today belongs to you … learn to like others on their own not
> for what they own.

Good Morning:

Sometimes we discover in life that wen we are poor in the things
of this world, we are rich in friendships.
For having less, we share more and it is in sharing that
friendship is shown.

> <u>Today belongs to you</u> ... take time to share ...
>   that a friend may know you care.

Good Morning:

The challenge of life is not in the desire to simply get by
but to prevent life from getting by you.
The desire to live every moment of life to the fullest,
not just to survive, but to be fully alive.

> <u>Today belongs to you</u> ... launch forth into it with new
>   excitement for everything you do.

Good Morning:

Happiness is life is not so much doing with you like as it is
in liking what you do ... in finding pleasure in those day to day
challenges that constantly confront us.

> <u>Today belongs to you</u> ... seek the happiness that lies hidden even
>   in the routine things you have to do.

Good Morning:

We never find ourselves by pursuing ourselves …
but only by seeking something greater than what we are …
until we discover that in following our dreams, we find ourselves.

Today belongs to you … pursue until your dreams come true.

Good Morning:

The greatest enjoyment we can get in life lies in the
pleasure of giving enjoyment to others. For pure enjoyment
is the one thing you can't get without also giving … for it is in the
giving of enjoyment that we in turn, become enjoyable.
Today belongs to you … use part of the day to
give some enjoyment away!

Good Morning:

The secret of success is in making the right decisions in life.
The secret of making the right decisions lies in experience.
The secret of gaining experience comes from making wrong
decisions.
Today belongs to you … remember, that even your wrong
decisions are rungs in the ladder of
success.

The Turbulent Ganges River

The Ganges is the longest and most sacred of all the rivers in India as well as the lifeblood of the Hindu religion. Hindus believe that bathing in the Ganges provides forgiveness for all of one's sins in this life and the next. Unlike Christianity, which believes in the life of Jesus Christ as detailed in the Bible, Hindus believe that there are many Gods to be worshipped.

The following quote from the Gospel of Thomas has proven to be one of the most memorable and important of all the discoveries I made while trekking the Himalayas.

After quoting the words of Jesus, "The Kingdom of God is within you." (Luke 17:21 NRSV)

St. Thomas goes on to say:

> *"If you bring forth what is within you, what you bring forth will save you.*
> *If you do not bring forth what is within you, what you do not bring forth will destroy you." (Gospel of Thomas 70:1-2)*

I wish I had learned that lesson earlier in life!

Good Morning:

Resolving life's problems comes about by working them out
Often we work them out by talking them through,
When we share the thoughts of our every worry and fear
We discover that new solutions suddenly appear.

<u>Today Belongs To You</u> share the thoughts of what you most fear
with those whom you hold most dear.

Good Morning:

Although our country was founded upon the concept of human freedom,
what most people really want more than freedom is a sense of security.
That is to be free think freely about new challenges, new ideas, new
thoughts.
To be able to feel secure in their own minds.

<u>Today Belongs To You</u>…Let freedom ring true through you.

Good Morning:

Life's victories are more often won through inspiration rather than
though one's natural abilities or skills. Our victories are more
often achieved through determination rather than chance, luck, or
whatever you will.

<u>Today Belongs To You</u>…Let your inspiration fuel your determination

Good Morning:

Sometimes it's more important to stretch your vision
    than it is to broaden your horizon;
For horizons have limits,
    but visions are as limitless as the human imagination.

Today Belongs To You… Let your imagination run beyond the
                    horizon.

Good Morning:

We give little when we give of what we own – when we give of our
possessions,
    the things of this world.
It's only when we give of ourselves that we give of what we uniquely
possess.

Today Belongs To You … let your relationships with others today
                    express the uniqueness of the personality
                    that only you possess.

Good Morning:

Too many daisies aren't enough
when you enjoy the beauty that they bring;
Too many hours aren't enough
when you are enjoying whatever you're doing;
Too many friends aren't enough
when you enjoy each and every one of them;

Today Belongs To You… Don't be afraid to indulge
                    and enjoy life with those whom you love.

Good Morning:

There is no such thing in life as a bad experience. All of life is
an experience... and whether it's good or bad depends not on
the experience, but rather on your interpretation of it.

<u>Today Belongs To You ...</u> view each of its experiences in a positive way.

Good Morning:

Contrary to the compulsion to make every minute count
It's more important sometimes to waste a little time...
Not to take yourself or your life too seriously
And to enjoy the life that God has given you.

<u>Today Belongs To You...</u> Enjoy it today in any way you choose.

Good Morning:

It's impossible to forgive if you can't forget
And it's impossible to forget if you can't forgive:
Without forgiveness your future is but an echo of the past
Of reliving old hurts and grudges that that shouldn't last

<u>Today Belongs To You ... try to</u> forgive those who have hurt you.

Good Morning:

It's not enough to have books on your bookshelves
You have to read them to acquire the knowledge you seek to attain;
It's not enough to watch life as it goes by every day
You have to wade into its flow and be a part of the fray.

Today Belongs To You. Jump right in with both feet
                and enjoy all those whom you'll meet.

Good Morning:

There are some things that can never be capture or contained
Yet which can be yours forever to remember and keep;
A moment of joy…the touch of love…the smell of a rose
The sun's glow in the morning that wakes you from sleep.

Today Belongs To You … Cherish those moments of rapture
               Which only the heart can capture.

Good Morning:

Some people complain because God put thorns among the roses.
Other people are thankful that there are roses to be found among
the thorns.

Today Belongs To You… Don't let the thorns keep you from
               smelling the roses.

Good Morning:

Success is not measured by the status you've obtained or the wealth
you've achieved
As much as it's measured by the number of obstacles you've overcome
along the way.

Today Belongs To You. … It's not something you receive
but rather it's something you achieve.

Good Morning:

Life is a gift – received at birth without our asking,
Love is a gift – received as a gift without our asking,
Today is a gift – received at dawn without our asking.

Today Belongs To You… it's a gift of life and love for you to enjoy.

Good Morning:

When you put your life on the line for something you believe in
There's always the possibility that you might not win.
But it's always a rewarding, refreshing and authentic experience
To face life's challenges with that kind of confidence.

Today Belongs To You. Believing you'll win gives you the
confidence to begin.

Good Morning:

There's nothing in this world that can be compared
To the joy that is fulfilled when that same joy is shared;
    And there is no greater pain ever to be known
    Than a sorrow that is carried all alone.

Today Belongs To You ... As joys are doubled in the sharing,
                    So sorrows are halved when you know
                    how much others are caring.

Good Morning:

I like the story of the little boy who had a black eye and when asked who gave it to him, he replied, "Nobody gave it to me. I had to fight for it." Life is often like that....and there are still things worth fighting for.

Today belongs to you ... and don't worry if you get a black eye or two.

Good Morning:

If love fills your heart, you'll find that there's no room left for hate. So this morning at today's start, let love be your primary trait.

Today belongs to you... Let love flow in and watch hate ebb away.

Good Morning:

The desire to appease often serves to satisfy those who demand you to please them.
However, if you desire to please someone then that desire gives pleasure to both the one that gives and the one that receives.

<u>Today belongs to you...</u> make it a pleasurable day !

Good Morning:

You can't make an omelet without breaking some eggs,
Nor can you make a decision without stepping on somebody's toes;
    And sometimes the decisions that you make
    Are ones that also make you feel that your own heart will break.
<u>Today belongs to you...</u> May the decisions you make
                  bring you success in everything you
                  undertake.

Visions and Dreams at Patmos

In the book of Acts 2:17 NRSV we read God's promise that *"In the last days … your young men* will see visions, and your old men shall dream dreams."* It's no wonder that I couldn't wait to drop anchor at Patmos harbor and to then quickly wend my way up this hillside to the cave where St. John wrote the book of Revelation which is the most memorable account of the Vision he had received from God.

I arrived in time to attend a vesper service at the cave. During its brief liturgy as I sat listening at the edge of the cave and looked out over the Aegean Sea. I could visualize St. John spending his days in isolation at that location listening for the Word of God. I was mortified when I realized that in my life I had rarely spent much quiet time listening for God to speak to me. I knew that I should have heeded his command to "Be still and know that I am God" but for all my years I was too busy writing words that I would be speaking from the pulpit to others on Sunday. *You can't talk and listen at the same time* and I resolved that evening to "be still" more often in the future hope of someday receiving a vision or a dream myself.

After this last chapter about sailing to Patmos and the occurring of dreams and visions I need to include this article I recently wrote about the only time I experienced what I would call a vision in my own life.

"I'd Know that Laugh Anywhere"

I was visiting daughter Karen in Minneapolis and decided to stay for the weekend which provided me with the opportunity to attend church at Westminster Presbyterian Church on Sunday morning where you can always depend upon hearing a sound sermon there as well as a commanding organ refrain. We sat in the balcony so that I could enjoy a commanding view of the congregation with the hope of seeing someone I might recognize even though it's been almost 40 years since I served the Rochester church in that Minnesota Presbytery. No such luck. However, my mind did enjoy the memory of past moments at Westminster and all the great homileticians who had so brilliantly preached from that massive pulpit.

After the worship service was over, we walked out the front door of the church onto the sidewalk where others were gathering and visiting and Karen said something that amused me and caused me to burst out laughing. Seconds later I heard a voice behind saying, "I'd know that laugh anywhere!" I turned and saw Rev. Max Maguire who years ago was the Dean of the CPE program located in Rochester First Presbyterian Church adjacent to the Mayo Clinic. Max was one of the ministers I most admired during my 19-year tenure when I occupied the Rochester pulpit. In seeing one another after so many years we both laughed instantly and embraced immediately to reconnect and revive happy memories of the past.

Later, on the way home, Karen said that while she was growing up and in high school the thing she enjoyed most about church was the laughter and the embracing that she witnessed every week at the church door as people departed to leave for home. She said that she used to wonder about it because she never read in the Bible that Jesus ever laughed but that I always did. She was aware that Jesus ate, that he drank wine, that he healed, that he preached, that he prayed, and even that he cried. But nowhere in scripture do we ever read that he laughed. Karen has always been an authentic critic of worship services and I have always taken her observations most seriously. Consequently I began thinking about her observation and comments regarding laughter and about the encounter Max and I had enjoyed at Westminster and the strong bonding that laughter engenders and which lasts beyond the years. In my experience I have learned that the people with whom I have come to love and trust the most are those with whom I have laughed the most. Laughter, I've come to believe, is the strengthening bond which allows us to feel comfortable in each other's presence and which leads us into the intimacy of faith and trust.

Recently I have been reading and rereading the Gospels discovered at Nag Hamadi and focusing mostly on Thomas and Judas. I enjoyed comparing their lives with the lives of the 21 Elders that were serving on the Session I was moderating. In our Church Sessions as well as in our national Boards and Agencies it appears to me that we elect the people whom we trust the most to be our treasurers and those with whom we have laughed the most we elect to positions of trust and leadership. Among the disciples it was Judas whom they all trusted with the position of 'Treasurer' (in charge of the purse) and a careful reading of his Gospel reveals that his relationship to Christ was the most intimate of any of his disciples. In reading the Gospel of Judas over and over again we cannot help noticing how often Jesus 'laughed' as he responded to the questions that Judas put to him. It was not a laughter of criticism but a laughter of enjoying the opportunity to share in the queries. In **13** brief pages we read that 'Jesus laughed' **9** times and while he was talking to his disciples. It was only Judas who had the courage to speak up and confront Jesus with the intimate questions of life which allowed them to converse on a level that the other disciples didn't understand. They had shared secrets which concerned the coming of the Kingdom of God.

I must share a dream that I had recently. Yes, I believe in dreams. I was walking with Jesus out on an old country road. Just quietly walking and talking. Dreams often give me new insights as to where my life should be going. After some time of listening I looked at him and I thought I sensed a smile coming across his face.

It looked like He was half-smiling at me. We walked on with our pace slowing a bit. Then while we were discussing whatever it was that was on our minds, I thought I heard what sounded like a muffled laugh. I couldn't contain my curiosity. I stopped and turned toward Him I said, "Are you laughing?"

"Yes" he answered "but it wasn't anything you said. Just an old memory….and the pleasure of being here."

We went on talking. I still don't remember what the subject was but I do remember that it was sprinkled with laughter until it finally ended with the two of us stopping right there in the middle of that country road looking at one another, laughing heartily and then embracing just for the pure pleasure of being in each other's presence. Then I woke up.

My laughter in my sleep had already awakened my wife Barb who wondered why my face was so radiant. My only answer was that I had just experienced the most ethereal moment of my life and all we had done was to laugh together.

Good Morning:

Defeat makes you either bitter or better.
It doesn't make you bitter if you don't swallow it.
It won't make you better if you don't learn from it.
<u>Today belongs to you</u> ...dare to accept defeat not as a bitter
pill to swallow, but as a bit of a thrill
in the journey of life we follow.

Good Morning:

You can blame luck for accidents ... but
you can't give it credit for success. For success is
Often not so much a matter of luck as it is the
result of the discipline of continued self-development
and self-fulfillment.
<u>Today belongs to you</u> ... don't waits for lady luck to do for you
what you have to do for yourself.

Good Morning:

Happiness in life is not something you experience as much as
it is something you remember. Therefore, the pursuit of happiness
is not a dream of the future as much as it is an appreciation of
the past.
<u>Today belongs to you</u> ... enjoy it to the point that the
memory of today may be tomorrow's
happiness.

Good Morning:

Getting the most out of life demands a great amount of patience.
You know that you don't get a chicken by smashing an egg …
but by hatching it, and that takes time.

> Today belongs to you … to get the most out of it before it
> ends, exercise a little patience with
> yourself and with your friends.

Good Morning:

Success in life is often dependent upon risking present security
for a new opportunity. The desire for security always
stands in the way of every new opportunity until you learn
that true security in life comes not from what you possess …
as much as from what you are!

> Today belongs to you … dare to risk something of what you
> are for what you want to be.

Good Morning:

The romance of life lies in the mystery of the unknown …
the unexpected …the ring of the phone … a letter in the mail …
the knock on the door … all moments to be greeted with
anticipation and high expectation.

> Today belongs to you … don't be afraid to accept the
> unexpected.

Good Morning:

Thanksgiving is not a holiday nor a season as much as
it is an attitude, a human reason for our gratitude …
a time to gather our thoughts as well as to
gather together as families and friends.
    <u>Today belongs to you</u> … take time to be thoughtful of that for
which you're thankful.

Good Morning:

Very often in life when we think we are only wasting time …
killing time, we are in truth really wasting ourselves …
killing our best opportunities for the future … and the
dreams we envision die before they are born.
    <u>Today belongs to you</u> … use today's time to begin making
tomorrow's dreams come true.

Good Morning:

Life was never meant to be held back
but to be free to flow forward …
not to be lost in the fear of living, but to be
found in the sheer excitement of beginning
a new day.
    <u>Today belongs to you</u> … don't for a moment ever
Repress the joy of life you want to
express!

Good Morning:

To have hope is to see success where others see failure,
to see sunshine where others see shadows and
to see light where others see darkness.
For there is no medicine known today that is as
powerful as hope.
     Today belongs to you ... hope for the best and don't worry
                              about the rest.

Good Morning:

To be kind in what you say is to create confidence.
To be kind in what you do is to create trust.
To be kind in what you think is to create love.
     Today belongs to you ...use today to let your kindness shine
                              through.

Good Morning:

A friend is someone with whom you choose to spend your time.
A *good* friend is someone with whom you choose to
spend your treasures. But a *best* friend is someone with whom
you choose to spend yourself.
     Today belongs to you ... let its best dividend be the time you
                              spend with your best friend.

Good Morning:

Our desire in life for temporary things often destroys our ultimate concern for others. Our dependence in life on temporal things often destroys our confidence in ourselves.

> <u>Today belongs to you</u> … work today, not to acquire things, but to aspire to possess the real treasures that life brings.

Good Morning:

Everybody wants to change the world … to change humanity. But in our own vanity, we never want to change ourselves.

> <u>Today belongs to you</u> … if you want to change the world, begin with a few small changes in your own life and then watch your world change too!

Good Morning:

Sometimes listening is more important than speaking and more hearts are moved by an open ear than be an open mouth. True listening draws hearts closer together than all the words that love can speak.

> <u>Today belongs to you</u> … listen with love as you share this day with those whom you live and love.

Good Morning:

Sometimes problems in life that can't be solved
    can with patience and understanding be resolved.
The danger of seeking the perfect solution to life's problems
is that we often ignore the simple and practical resolutions.
    Today belongs to you … remember that there is no problem in
        life that cannot be resolved!

Good Morning:

Success in life often lies not in giving the right answers
as much as it is in knowing the right questions.
Sometimes questioning old ideas leads to the discovery
of new ideas and, in turn, a better way of doing things.
    Today belongs to you … don't be afraid to try something new.

Good Morning:

Christmas giving at its best is child-like in its spontaneity.
It is not counting the cost but delighting in seeing the
    pleasure that the gift brings to others.
    Today belongs to you …let the spontaneity of your giving be
        the added value to your gift.

Footloose on Mt. Fuji

One evening I mentioned to my wife Barbara that of all the mountains, (Himalayas, Alps Olympus, Sinai, Rockies) and rivers (Amazon, Nile, Ganges, Mississippi) and historic sites that I had traveled to, I regretted that I had never been to Japan. Not surprisingly, Barbara's response was "Let's go!" So, we did.

After visiting the religious, cultural and historic locales we had planned to take time to climb the Japanese sacred Mount Fuji. We took the 'Bullet train' from Tokyo to the base of the mountain and began our climb. The misty rain made the trail a bit treacherous inasmuch as the many stones and pebbles we walked over were wet which made the path quite slippery. More than once we fell down and had to have the help of the other to get up. By the time we were half-way up the mountainside we were both exhausted as much from laughter at our constant falling as from the physical demands of climbing and helping each other stand up after a slip or fall.

Ecclesiastes puts it: "Two are better than one, For if they fall, one will lift up the other" (Eccl. 4:9 NRSV) That's what we remember of that climb....and what we now cherish as the framed needlepoint text of our marriage.

Good Morning:

When we tape this TV show, the one thing I can do
is to ask for a re-take when I blow a line.
But life has no re-takes ... there are no chances to edit out
life's mistakes or to erase a single moment.
    Today belongs to you ... live to fulfill its every
    Intent rather than trying to change a past event.

Good Morning:

There is nothing to fear as we look forward to a new year.
There is nothing to dread as we look toward the days ahead ...
For the dream of the future is always better than living in the past.
    Today belongs to you ...believe that dreams will come true.

Good Morning:

The old year is past and the new year is here.
Let forgiveness be your only link with the past and
let love be your only link to the future.
    This year belongs to you ... don't let what's old
                    tarnish what's new.

Good Morning:

As the new year begins, we think we have time enough to
spend and to spare. But as each day ends, we realize how
Precious little time we've had to share.
And though the years may seem eternal, we live day by day
And morning all to soon becomes nocturnal.
    Today belongs to you … spare some time to share.

Good Morning:

Sometimes a new idea strikes just the right key to
unlock suppressed desires to fulfill a dream… a secret
ambition. So that the dream becomes reality and
ambition becomes success.
    Today belongs to you … don't be afraid to explore
                        Some new challenge you've never
                        tried before.

Good Morning:

As you face this day with all its demands, don't let your
schedule be so full that there isn't time for yourself.
But let your life be flexible even though the hours are
inexorable.
    Today belongs to you … be as open to the day
                        as the day is to you.

Good Morning:

To be helpful is to anticipate the needs of others.
To be thoughtful is to anticipate the desires of others.
But to be sensitive is to anticipate the feelings of others.
<u>Today belongs to you</u> ... let your sensitivity to others direct
whatever you do.

Good Morning:

A decision postponed is a decision you have to make twice.
And not to decide is to let someone else decide for you.
Therefore, it's better to take action in life
than to let life force its actions upon you.
<u>Today belongs to you</u> ... don't be afraid to make
your own decision and then do
whatever you have to do.

Good Morning:

It's often hard in life to stand up for your convictions,
To stand by your principles. Just as it's hard to risk
what you are for what you want to be.
<u>Today belongs to you</u> ... remembers; if you don't
fight for a principle, life soon loses its
interest.

Good Morning:

Nothing we do can ever be accomplished alone …
if not done *for* another, it must be done *with* another…
or at least *in the context* of others who
share the world with us.
 <u>Today belongs to you</u> … but is also belongs to
 others too …. share it.

Good Morning:

Victory in life is to be vanquished and yet not surrender,
to be beaten and yet not to give up,
to be defeated and yet not to stop trying.
For the victorious life is in its triumph over stress and strife.
 <u>Today belongs to you</u> … never give up what
 You've set your heart to do.

Good Morning:

Confidence comes from within … from your belief in yourself …
from knowing that your abilities are as great as life's opportunities,
and your capabilities are as great as life's challenges.
 <u>Today belongs you</u> … trust your self-confidence to carry you
 through.

Good Morning:

Uniqueness is the most personal of all our human qualities
and one of the most important; whereas conformity
is often the most demeaning.
For every soul, like a star, has its own special sparkle that
sets it apart from all others.
    <u>Today belongs to you</u> ... don't be afraid to be
                       the star you are!

Good Morning:

Success in life lies in
turning your liabilities into assets,
turning your mistakes into learning experiences, and
turning lemons into lemonade.
    <u>Today belongs to you</u> ... let the sum of everything
                       that's a minus add up in your life to
                       be a plus.

Good Morning:

The word you don't speak ... the feeling you don't share
never allows others to know how much you care.
And apologies thought yet never spoken
never heal a heart that is broken
    <u>Today belongs to you</u> ... don't be afraid to speak
                       from the heart and to let your true
                       feelings
                       show through.

Good Morning:

A diamond can't be polished without friction.
Nor a person perfected without experiencing some affliction.
For it is only under fire that gold is refined and
Only under pressure that diamonds are mined.
    Today belongs to you ... let even its pressures
                        Bring out the best in all that you do.

Good Morning:

Opposition is sometimes opportunity in disguise
For opposition often causes us to open our eyes
to new possibilities in different directions
as life moves forward.
    Today belongs to you ... let every adversity be a new door for
                        you to walk through.

Good Morning:

It's not how a book begins but how it ends that makes it memorable.
It's not how a job begins but how it ends that gives us satisfaction.
It's not how a day begins but how it ends that leaves us fulfilled.
    Today belongs to you ... and no matter how it begins
                    how it ends depends on what you do.

I Owe Iona a Debt of Thanks

When I was a student at the University of Glasgow I mentored under the world reknown Dr. Wm. Barclay who one day, after we had come to know each other quite well, took me aside after class and said that I often appeared to him to act more like a politician at Parliament seeking re-election than a minister seeking to preach and proclaim the Gospel. He was right. I needed some time to be alone and time for meditative introspection Then he surprisingly added that he had made reservations through the Headmaster at the Iona Study

Center for me to spend a weekend there. I was humbly thankful for his observation of my ministerial lifestyle but not at all excited or anxious to go to Iona, a well known monastic styled study center on a small (1 mile by 3 mile) in the Hebrides of Northern Scotland.

The next Friday I left for Iona. It was a long half day's journey. I didn't want to go there, but I couldn't get over Dr. Barclays observations of my lifestyle and his genuine concern for my spiritual well being which superceded any anxiety over my academic achievements. He wanted me to learn the necessity of a silent and tranquil relationship with the Christ whom I preached about to others.

Dr. Barclay's advice and guidance proved to have a life changing affect on my life. His willingness to mentor me and helped me overcome my ambition to become a 'popular preacher'. It was a lesson I needed to learn…and I realized how deeply in debt I was for his teaching me that my role as a pastor was not the goal to be popular and loved by my congregation but rather it should be for me to learn to love my congregation.

Good Morning:

When asked about his ancestry, Abraham Lincoln once said,
"I don't know who my grandfather was, but I am much
more concerned to know what his grandson will be."
    <u>Today belongs to you</u> ... rather than depending upon past
ancestry, make every effort to
prepare for today's opportunity.

Good Morning:

On this morning after Valentine's Day ... after you've given gifts
of love to others, take some time to be generous to yourself.
For even a Valentine knows that it's in the giving and not
in the getting that love slowly grows.
    <u>Today belongs to you</u> ... you can't love others unless you also
love yourself.

Good Morning:

We are often tempted to try to see what lies ahead of us
At the end of the day that we fail to see clearly what work
lies right before us as the day begins. We are often so
concerned about the big jobs ahead that we
don't begin the little jobs at hand.
    <u>Today belongs to you</u> ... take it one step at a time.

Good Morning:

The only limits that are set upon what we can do in this
world are the limits of fear that we set for ourselves ...
fear of something or someone which destroys our
Confidence in ourselves.
    <u>Today belongs to you</u> ... concentrate today on your capacity
                        for success and discover the limitless
                        abilities that you possess.

Good Morning:

Innovators and creators are persons who to an extreme degree
Are willing to follow their own visions and their own dreams ...
Even if they're led in the opposite direction of life's mainstream.
For the secret of creativity is simply the courage to dare to do.
    <u>Today belongs to you</u> ... so say it again ... I do, I do, I do!

Good Morning:

When you're always on the run with things to do and
meetings to attend, you sometimes don't even
have a moment to meet yourself ... coming or going!
Yet we all need times of quiet to meet ourselves
where we are going.
    <u>Today belongs to you</u> ... take time to
                      revitalize your life.

Good Morning:

Life is motion and not to move forward is ultimately
to move backward. For life goes on and to stand still
is to be left behind.
<u>Today belongs to you</u> ... and since the day isn't something you
can hold back or capture, live it with
enthusiasm, excitement and rapture!

Good Morning:

Life comes to you ... fresh as a daisy and new every morning.
To live it to its capacity is to meet it with spontaneity and
to accept the excitement of all that's unexpected and
follow its direction in ways you never suspected.
<u>Today belongs to you</u> ... fresh as a daisy and picked just for you.

Good Morning:

Our greatest hope for a sense of permanence and continuity
in life depends upon our ability to handle the changes we
confront each day. For enthusiasm in life endures only when
we decide not to fight the flow of life but
to learn to grow with each new challenge.
<u>Today belongs to you</u> ... follow the flow and gain momentum
as you go.

Good Morning:

It takes time to plan for things in the future
It takes time for all things to slowly mature
It takes time to grow in wisdom and stature
It takes time to gain strength to quietly endure.
    <u>Today belongs to you</u> … be patient in all that you do.

Good Morning:

We gain confidence in life through every difficult experience
that we survive. But more than surviving, difficult experiences
transform us so that experience upon experience
we gain confidence for the furture.
    <u>Today belongs to you</u> … remember that the difficult experiences
                                you encounter today empower you with
                                confidence for tomorrow.

Good Morning:

It's not how much you have but how much you want that makes
you rich or poor. For he who has little and wants more is poor and
he who has much and still wants more is also poor.
    <u>Today belongs to you</u> … remember that happiness is not
                                in having what you want, but in
                                wanting what you have.

Good Morning:

The essentials for happiness in life are:
something to do, someone to love and
something to hope for.
For having something to do gives you purpose,
having someone to love gives life fulfillment, and
having something to hope for gives life meaning.
    <u>Today belongs to you</u> ... let your happiness be found in
                         something you do, someone you love
                         and something you've hoped for.

Good Morning:

Beauty is not something you find in the world ... rather it is
something you are in the world. For beauty is not so much in
what you behold as it is in the heart where you let love unfold.
    <u>Today belongs to you</u> ... be the beautiful person that you are.

Good Morning:

St. Patrick may represent the luck of the Irish ... but life is
More than luck ... more than being dealt a good hand.
The good life often lies in being able to play a poor hand well!
    <u>Today belongs to you</u> ... play it out with finesse.

Good Morning:

Let your identity in life be ... not in what surrounds you
Aa much as in who you are and what you do.
For it's your inner life ... your hopes and dreams ...
that keep you from being a slave to your surroundings.
    <u>Today belongs to you</u> ... let your inner life shine through.

Good Morning:

Only if you truly like yourself can you enjoy the pleasure of
your own leisure. And only when you're with the person you
like best can you share these moments of leisure hours at rest.
For to enjoy your leisure is to also enjoy being who you are.
    <u>Today belongs to you</u> ... let your moments of leisure be the
                                    moments you treasure.

Good Morning:

Winning in life does not mean that someone else has to lose ...
it simply means that you have done your best to achieve a goal
that you have conceived ... and then to believe you deserve to win.
    <u>Today belongs to you</u> ... strive to realize every goal you've ever
                                    visualized.

Good Morning:

To be at peace with the world really means to be at peace
with yourself. And you can be at peace with yourself even if
your world is collapsing around you for peace comes from that
inner confidence that lets others in
rather than from those defenses we use to keep others out.

    <u>Today belongs to you</u> … if you are at peace with yourself you
will be at peace with others too.

Good Morning:

To care for someone is to carry a concern for them in your heart.
But to worry about someone is to create unnecessary anxiety
when you're apart.
For caring is the way that love is expressed
but to worry is to show fear of losing what you possess.

    <u>Today belongs to you</u> … let the energy you expend be the care
that you share for a friend.

Coming to America

Memories of coming to America stull haunt me. Our ship's loud speaker announced that the ETA was for early the next day. I was so excited that I could hardly sleep during the night. By morning I was the first one on deck ... standing alone, straining to see "by the dawn's early light." Soon I could make out the form of the Statue of Liberty as 'she so proudly hailed" all who passed her as we approached the Manhattan skyline. It was at that moment that fears of being detained at Ellis Island gripped my heart again. What if I had Tuberculosis? Or some other dreaded disease? Or what if this … or what if that? I was terrified by the thought of being separated from my family in a new and strange country. I am sure that my parents had no idea of the fears that I was experiencing. They were concerned with matters of disembarkation and I was terrified by thoughts of deportation.

The point of all of this is that what I remembered of that morning is not what I **saw,** but what I **felt.** I couldn't tell you if it had been a sunny day or a cloudy day. I don't remember the date on the calendar, but I can never forget the feelings in my heart as I approached this new juncture in my life. I learned a very important lesson in life that day. **What truly matters in life is not what you see but what you feel.** And nowadays whenever I hear the National Anthem played publicly and the crowds start singing, "Oh, Say, can you see?" I want to shout out, *"No, No, It's not what you **see,** but what you **feel** about your country that's important!"*

Jesus doesn't ask us to behold Him but only to Love him!

Good Morning:

It's more important in life to run ahead in search of something
than it is to run away in fear of something.
For the successful life is goal oriented with visions clear
rather than disoriented with apprehensive fear.
     Today belongs to you ... seek and search for something
                                        new ... to be ... or to do.

Good Morning:

Success lies in action more than in knowledge ... for though
many people know what they'd like to do ... few there are
who dare to ... who have the courage to act out their dreams.
     Today belongs to you ... let your dreams be as real as they seem!

Good Morning:

Sometimes we look but don't see
and we hear but don't listen.
And it's usually because our expectations are
below our dreams and we become blind to the
obvious and deaf to the music that surrounds us.
     Today belongs to you ... keep at least one eye and an ear open
                                        to the possibility of your dreams
                                        coming true.

Good Morning:

We often forfeit the best in ourselves just to be like others
when, in fact, the most exciting aspect of your self is that
you are not like others.
But it takes courage to stand up for your own individuality
and to be vulnerable to yourself.
    <u>Today belongs to you</u> ... don't sacrifice the beauty that is you
just to live like others do.

Good Morning:

Success often demands sacrifice ...
the willingness to give up many things for something ...
or to give up everything for one thing.
Only you can decide what that something is worth ...
or what that one thing will be.
    <u>Today belongs to you</u> ... do one thing ... do it well and
success will be yours.

Good Morning:

On this first day of the week ... as you look ahead to
all there is to do, take a moment now to arrange your priorities
and separate the necessary from the unnecessary.
For there are some things you just don't have to do.
    <u>Today belongs to you</u> ... cut through the clutter of life ...
eat the wheat and laugh at the chaff.

Good Morning:

Greatness often lies not in doing extraordinary things
as much as in doing ordinary things and doing them
extraordinarily well using all your energy and enthusiasm
in facing the challenges this day brings.
Today belongs to you … the greatness belongs to you too!

Good Morning:

The problem in life is not in living above your means
as much as it is in living below your limits, below your potential
for life finds its fulfillment only in the unfolding of
your latent talents and unused powers.
Today belongs to you … unleash that potential that's waiting
to break through.

Good Morning:

A flawless flower often seems all too artificial.
The perfect gift often seems all to insincere.
For very often it's our flaws, the little imperfections in
our lives that create the differences that make us unique.
Today belongs to you … flaunt your flaws and let your
uniqueness shine through.

Good Morning:

Permanence is not always a measure of a things worth
or value for sometimes the most lasting pleasure if found
in life's fleeting moments … in brief encounters which
though quickly past are forever remembered.
　　Today belongs to you … enjoy its minutes as well the hours.

Good Morning:

Sometimes in the summer when the moon rises during
the daylight hours … even though it sheds very little light
its appearance is as spectacular as when it shines at night.
For its beauty is not in the light that the sunshine hides
as much as in the pleasure that the moon's ambience provides.
　　Today belongs to you … may it be filled with
　　　　　　　　　　　　pleasure …rising like moonlight in
　　　　　　　　　　　　the daylight.

Good Morning:

You can't shake hands with a clenched fist
Any more than you can hug someone
with your arms folded around yourself.
For to be open with others in spirit is also
to be open to them in fact,
　　Today belongs to you … meet it with open arms as well as an
　　　　　　　　　　　　open mind.

Good Morning:

More important in life than being great is being grateful,
being appreciative. For greatness cannot be achieved
without a concurring sense of thankfulness to those by
whose help your greatness has been realized.

    <u>Today belongs to you</u> ... before it ends, take some time to
                     express your appreciation to your
                     colleagues and friends.

Good Morning:

Doing unto others as you wish they would do unto you
may not be as golden as doing unto others as
<u>they may wish</u> you'd do unto them ... for their wishes
may not be the same as yours; and
what you want may not be what they want.

    <u>Today belongs to you</u> ... try to be as sensitive to the needs of
                     others as you are to your own.

Good Morning:

To own does not always mean to possess.
And to possess does not always mean to have as one's own.
For sometimes what we think we own ... in truth owns us
and what we think we possess is really that by which
we are possessed!

    <u>Today belongs to you</u> ... may it find you free from the stress of
                     worrying about the things you think
                     you possess.

Good Morning:

To love is to touch as if you possess … as much as to caress.
For to have does not necessarily mean to hold, for
even a flower held too tightly soon has its petals crushed.
    <u>Today belongs to you</u> … not to possess, but to enjoy.

Good Morning:

The unhappiest people in the world are the people
who fear change … who fear the progress that comes
with change. For change is the motivating factor that
generates progress and happiness comes in learning how
to be flexible while living in a world that is in a state of
perpetual flex.
    <u>Today belongs to you</u> … greet change as a chance to flex with
the flow.

Good Morning:

In this day and age when we are all concerned about
living above our means, our greater concern should be the
fear of living below our potential … of using only a
small part of our limitless abilities and capabilities. For
living within your means doesn't necessarily mean
living below your potential.
    <u>Today belongs to you</u> … don't let your liabilities limit your
potentialities.

Pondering at the Pyramids

I took my 18 year old daughter Kate on this trip down the Nile to ancient Egypt so that she could see the Pyramids. On our first morning we went to Giza to see the Sphinx We climbed the Pyramid of Khufu, the largest of them all and about half way up its side we entered inside the pyramid and walked through its interior on wooden planks until we came to the Kings burial chamber which is about in the middle of the pyramid. I had never suffered from claustrophobia before but I certainly did while I was within that burial site looking at that great burial vault.

After we emerged we took a short walk and came to a stable where they had horses to rent. So I rented one for Kate and she took off like a rocket riding across the desert dunes loving the free expanse of the endless desert and also having the freedom to think her own teenage thoughts. She needed the alone time to process in her mind what she had just experienced. That evening an outdoor restaurant provided just the right atmosphere to talk about our day and our own lives. We talked about life and death. I listened intently. Sitting there under the canopy of the stars with the Nile River (the Egyptian source of **life**) to my right and the Pyramids (the Egyptian symbols of **death**) to my left I couldn't help but recite (in my mind) the first sentence of the Presbyterian BRIEF STATEMENT OF FAITH which begins: *"In life and in death we belong to God"*.

Good Morning:

Let your first thoughts this morning be your best thoughts
for today ... and let your secret thoughts be your happiest
thoughts ... and don't let your second thoughts keep you
from fulfilling your best thoughts.

<u>Today belongs to you</u> ... and may your last thoughts tonight
make tomorrow's dreams come true.

Good Morning:

Each day has a newness about it. It's never a carbon copy
of yesterday. And what is new today can bring newness
into your life ... for growth comes with new visions and
new insights as one experience flows into another.

<u>Today belongs to you</u> ...let each experience help you grow as
you go with the flow.

Good Morning:

There's a difference between growing up in life and maturing ...
for where growing up is often simply growing taller,
maturing is growing wiser and forgiving ... growing sympathetic
and more loving.

<u>Today belongs to you</u> ... and remember that even when your
growing up is through, there's still
some growing you can do.

Good Morning:

One of the greatest discoveries you can make in life is to learn
that by changing your thoughts you can change your life. For we
are architects of our own destinies and it is by our choices that
we direct our own lives.

Today belongs to you ... and what you are thinking now is
what you'll probably do!

Good Morning:

When love and appreciation are something you
fail to express then even your friends are left having
to guess ... if the thanks they think you feel are feelings
that are really real.

Today belongs to you ... use a moment to show your thanks
to someone for something they've
done for you.

Good Morning:

Peace in the world comes no easier than the peace we
make with one another ... and being at peace with
one another is no easier than the peace we make with
ourselves. For to be at peace with oneself is to simultaneously
be at peace with the world.

Today belongs to you ... if you're at peace with yourself you'll
find yourself at peace with others too.

Good Morning:

Sometimes standing alone against the crowd is not so much an
act of defiance as an act of self-compliance ... of being true to
yourself. For there is no sense trying to live like the crowd if
being authentic means living by liking yourself.
<u>Today belongs to you</u> ... and to your own self be true.

Good Morning:

Graciousness is not in what we say or do
but rather in *how* we say what we say and *how* we do what we do.
For words often conceal what we really feel just as our
public deeds can often hide the private thoughts we hold inside.
<u>Today belongs to you</u> ... let graciousness find its way into all you do.

Good Morning:

Success never simply comes to you in life ...you have to meet it
at least half-way ... and that preparation is often the key
to your success ... which more often depends upon your own
readiness.
<u>Today belongs to you</u> ... use it to get ready for the future that
you'll someday walk into.

Good Morning:

Life isn't full unless it's filled with hope ...
    hope for yourself ... hope for tomorrow ...
    hope for others ...
for it is hope that helps you cope with life and
gives you enthusiasm and confidence for tomorrow.
    <u>Today belongs to you</u> ...may it be filled with such hope,
                    that yesterday's dreams will come true.

Good Morning:

Thanksgiving is more than just a day of gratitude. It is our public celebration of a personal attitude of dependence upon God our creator
and our interdependence upon one another.
    <u>Today belongs to you</u> ...
    enjoy one another and give thanks for that joy!

Good Morning:

Success in life often comes not in what we achieve or what we do
as much as in that happy feeling we experience when we have
helped someone else along life's way ... when we have helped others
to see their dreams come true.
    <u>Today belongs to you</u> ...and success does too ... when you
                  help other people through whatever
                  you do.

Good Morning:

To be in love with life is to love all of life. To have
zest for life is to have enthusiasm for all of life ... not just
the good things and the good days ... but all things and every day.
Today belongs to you ... and if you love it, it will return love
to you.

Good Morning:

Tact is often simply the knack of keeping quiet at the right time.
Sometimes that means that you simply don't over-react and
instead you become sensitive to others so that they, in turn,
become sensitive too.
Today belongs to you ... convert your reactions into tactful actions.

Good Morning:

Everybody wants to change the world ... and all to the better.
But we rarely want to begin that change with ourselves.
We can see how other people should change and
we're often eager to give them suggestions;
while at the same time we're reluctant to
take any constructive corrections!
Today belongs to you ... and in the course of the day don't be
afraid to let change affect you.

Good Morning:

Being different in what we are and who we are does not necessarily
mean that we have to be divisive ... for it is in our uniqueness ...
our little differences that life becomes exciting. For unity
does not necessarily mean uniformity.

<u>Today belongs to you</u> ... and even you can disagree without
being disagreeable.

Good Morning:

Fear is the greatest enemy of mankind ... and the slightest threat
to our security plunges us into panic and we lose faith in ourselves
and in the future. However, the truth is that we all have
reserve strength and power enough to see us through and
tragedy we might meet.

<u>Today belongs to you</u> ... and let your confidence conquer your
fears.

Good Morning:

Absence often makes the heart grow fonder
but then, they also say out of sight and out of mind.
Whatever may be your case today, let heart and thought
be together entwined.

<u>Today belongs to you</u> ... let your heart lead your mind to
thoughts of others ever loving, ever
kind.

The Soul Stirring Sahara

One of the great writers of a desert experience was Antoine de Saint-Exupery the great French novelist and aviator won the French "Legion d'honneur" during the 2nd World War. Earlier, in 1935 his plane crashed in the Sahara Desert and out of that near death experience he later developed **the story** of "The Little Prince" which has long been one of my favorite volumes. It has been translated into over 250 languages and dialects and. It was his earlier book, "Wind Sand and Stars" (a desert Journal) that motivated me later in life to motorcycle across the Sahara desert in order to share something of that desert experience . Daughter Karen knew how much my life was inspired by Saint-Exupery and when she was in High School she hand printed and framed this memorable quote for me from "The Little Prince" and it is still on my desk today. "It is only with the heart that can one see rightly, what is essential is invisible to the eye." I still hold that to be one of the great truths of life. *It's not what you see or know, but what you feel in your heart that's important.*

Jesus made this same observation in the last chapter of John's Gospel. After his resurrection Jesus appeared to his disciples on the shoreline of the Sea of Galilee. There he shared a breakfast of bread and fish with them and then he looked at Simon Peter and he said, "Simon, do you Love me?" (John 21:15-17 NRSV) Three times he asked Peter the same question. It was the ultimate question of Life. Jesus didn't ask Peter if he had memorized all the answers to the questions in the Catechism, or if he understood all the Doctrines of the church, or if he could explain the mystery of the miracles that he had seen. It was a question that only the heart could answer. "Do you love me? In fact, I recently told Barb that I don't want a resplendent funeral with an inflated obituary in the newspaper when I die, recounting all the things that I have seen in this world or done in this life. I simply want it to say in St. Peter's words, "Lord, you know that I love you."

An Addendum

I can't let this book go without adding a personal note lest you think that I live in a Poyllyannish world that denies all the tragedies and realities that one faces every day in life.

I know that all of these motivational vignettes that I have conjured and written in this volume are in reality no more than emotional bandaids to give you a momentary boost every morning as your start the day. They serve only as a crutch to help get you through the tough times and to help you put a smile on your face as you begin your day.

The Bible isn't about such trivialities. The Bible offers us an understanding of the deeper concerns of life and death and eternity. Now at 91 years of age it is to those concerns that I have focused my attention. Learning how to die is not an easy task and the Bible is your best enabler.

It was while I was writing these motivational tid-bits that my brother (A Surgeon) came to visit and get a final opinion on his cancer at the Mayo Clinic. The doctors told him that he had a month or so to live. I visited him in his hospital room the day he was scheduled to fly back home to Oregon.

We talked for a while. Mostly loving memories. Then it was time for me leave. We stood up at his bedside. He was in his hospital gown. We embraced for the last time in this life. Neither of us would let go of the other. His wife split us apart and I walked out the door and down the corridor. I came to the elevator. Pushed the 'down' button and then I physically collapsed. My back was against the wall and I slowly slid down to the floor, sat there and cried...and cried. I still haven't emotionally overcome that moment. We had grown up together on the Mission field in Lebanon and now I couldn't believe that it was all over. His death had completely drained the life out of me. I couldn't even write anything uplifting for anyone anymore.

I share this to remind you that life's sorrows are enduring and I don't want you to think that a few motivational vignettes can change the reality of the sorrows that we experience. When I was the pastor of a large Presbyterian church across the street from the Mayo Clinic for 19 years I had the opportunity to have many Mayo physicians as my friends. One day as some of us were sitting around a lunch table at the University Club one of my friends upon hearing that I would soon be resigning after all those years said to me "You're going to miss all of this after you leave." I responded, "I know, but I will be so relieved to be gone and know that I won't have to bury any of you."

Funerals, for me have been very difficult. Especially when you have become bonded to a congregation. I cannot do a funeral without being reminded of the words of the 17th Century cleric John Donne, dean of St. Paul's Cathedral in London in 1623 who wrote "Any man's death diminishes me because I am involved in Mankind. And therefore never send to know for whom for bell tolls: it tolls for thee." (No Man is an Island 1624)

I understand that and I still remember how much my brother's death diminished me.

I write this because I don't want you to feel that these vignettes which I have written are trite or flippant. I wrote this book 40 years ago, but it has taken me this long to publish it. It helped me work through a difficult time in my own life, but it is not intended to be a panacea for life's deeper problems. However, now nearing death myself I have decided to share it with you.

I do hope that you'll enjoy it.

No Longer Possessed by What I No Longer Possess

"One's life does not consist in the abundance of one's possessions." Luke 12:15 NRSV

A certain man and his wife from the city of Gadara, the capital city of the region of Decapolis, walked out of the front door of their palatial home, after a leisurely lunch, paused on their veranda, glanced out over the vast acreages that they owned and began talking to each other about the possibility of buying even more land in order to provide even more room for their ever increasing swine herd. The steep cliffs one side of their property had for generations provided them the protection that they needed to preserve and defend their inheritance through hundreds of years against countless invading armies. Living on such a protected plateau East of the Jordan River also gave them a strong sense of security which allowed them to conduct their business affairs with a sense of confidence that they could save their accumulated wealth over the years and put it aside as an inheritance for future generations. The region of Decapolis consisted of a large Greek and Roman citizenry and being swine herders was a very profitable occupation for a Gentile population which enjoyed the taste of pork and bacon. In that country they were known as 'Swine-herders' and frankly we were quite well off and more than proud of the size of our herd which had grown considerably over the generations. It was difficult work, but it was honorable labor and recently it had proved to be more financially rewarding than ever before.

Later that afternoon the husband went out into the fields to check on his hired hands. His wife remained at home and kept thinking about the possibility of gaining more land. Later in life as she recounted the unexpected events of that day, she said, "It was in the month of September, as I remember, when our lives changed more spectacularly than if the Roman Army had scaled our chalk stone cliffs and invaded our seemingly secure homeland. It was late that afternoon when my husband looking totally exhausted came into the house and sat down in the atrium and looked up at me with an expression that I can best describe as one of fear embedded in anger and said, 'It's Over. We're done in. Our life is over. We're financially wiped out.' He kept repeating the words over and over again. He appeared to be in a state of shock. I called one of the servants to bring in some wine as I tried to slow down his ranting and raving but he was so upset that nothing he said made any sense. It sounded to me as though he was saying that our swine herd had all fallen off over the edge of the cliffs and drowned in the sea below. But swine instinctively never go near the cliff's edge and not one has ever accidentally fallen to its death. As our conversation progressed and as he regained his composure he told me and the servants that had gathered into the atrium that he had noticed that there was a man at the foot of the cliffs earlier in the day who had just come ashore from a sailing vessel and was speaking to a gathered crowd of intent listeners. He thought nothing of it until suddenly a wild man evidently obsessed with demons came charging into the group screaming and yelling. Right at that moment my husband heard a rumbling among his pigs and soon they were dashing about in every direction, grunting and snorting. Suddenly they seemed to have been herded by some unforeseen force and driven to the edge of our mesa. There they seemed to be obsessed by an unknown force and they collectively dashed over the edge of the high cliffs on the perimeter of our property and together they dashed down to their death on the sea shore below.

My husband couldn't hear or understand what was being said by any of the individuals in the crowd at the base of our cliffs, but he stated that all at once the half naked wild man who had been distracting and threatening the crowd below became subdued and soon sat down quietly at the speakers feet, listening as quietly as if he were one of members of the original gathering. My husband who was standing on the top edge of the cliffs remained immobilized staring off into space unable to understand what had just happened below him. At the same time he knowingly realized that he had just lost all that we ever owned. In an instant all our wealth had disappeared from his sight and he now stood alone in his distress. He had just been dispossessed of all the wealth that he had accumulated over his lifetime. His desperation caused him for a moment to think about jumping off the cliff himself. Some of his hired hands, seeing him in such a confused state of mind while he was standing there on the cliffs edge went over to him and helped him stagger back to our home where without saying a word to me they helped him gain a seat in our atrium. I couldn't believe the ashen look on his face. He appeared to have aged years since he left that morning. His eyes bore a depth of sadness greater than those who gathered to grieve at a funeral. Frantically I asked him what had happened. He made no response. He just looked with a blank stare out at the barren field where our swine herd used to freely roan each day.

The days went by and we began the process of trying to salvage what we could out of the debris of our despair. We put our beautiful and luxurious home up for sale. We put our land up for sale, but there were no buyers at all. Everyone was now afraid of buying cliffside property, fearing that the same fate and destruction would befall them that had befallen us. The very cliffs that had been our fortress and defense from outside intruders had now become the nemesis and ill omen that prevented the best realtors from wanting to list our property. Rumors of ruin and remorse quickly spread throughout the city. We soon found a small space in downtown Gadara that suited our new minimal needs and we moved what we hadn't sold into our new dwelling space.

The socio-economic challenge of such a change of venue was the first emotional shock wave we encountered. It was something of a reality check of life itself. Let me tell you, there is a world of difference between living in a palatial home surrounded by servants and hired hands serving you for their pay and living in a small apartment being surrounded by friends and loving neighbors ready to assist you at every turn simply for Love's sake.

I was beginning to learn that wealth has its drawbacks and its disadvantages. That wealth generates its own demons, the worst of which are that wealth provides us individually with a sense of self-sufficiency. If you have money you don't need anything else nor do you need ANYONE else.

It wasn't long before I began to realize that I was starting to enjoy living in our small cramped apartment. I also was growing accustomed to the fact that I had almost immediately lost my sense of self sufficiency as my husband and I began sharing in fulfilling life's chores together. I realized anew that there is a closeness that grows stronger whenever you share the simple things of life together.

Now it happened that one morning a neighbor of mine told me about a man who spoke regularly in the market place about an itinerant preacher named Jesus whom many called "The Messiah". In fact, my neighbor lady told me that at one time this preacher who was a follower of Jesus had been possessed by many demons and used to run around half naked creating havoc among the population that lived right below our famed cliffs. He said that the man called Jesus had driven the demons out of that man and that had changed his life miraculously. He had asked Jesus if he could join the band of disciples that traveled with him but Jesus denied him that privilege and instead Jesus gave him the challenge to remain in his own village and to become a "missionary disciple" in his own region around the countryside of Gadara. For that reason, he became a preacher and teacher who shared in the market place all that Jesus had ever told him or taught him. My neighbor lady said that the crowds listening to him had been growing daily. So immediately I made her promise that she would take me with her the next time she went to market. Secretly I couldn't wait.

It wasn't more than a day later that she knocked on my door and we were off to the market. It's not that I had anything to buy nor did I have extra money to spend on things I couldn't buy. I was just anxious to hear this disciple of Jesus. When I first saw him I couldn't begin to imagine that he had ever been a wild man possessed with many demons...so many that they were called 'Legion'. He was comfortably dressed and he seemed very comfortable in speaking to the gathered assembly. He was thoughtful and not accusatory. He began by telling about the demons that had possessed him and how important it was to recognize your demons or else they will possess you without your knowing it. On my first morning listening to him he told a story which he called a 'parable' that Jesus used to explain the danger of succumbing to the Demon of Greed. He quoted Jesus as saying:

"One's life does not consist of one's possessions" (Luke 12:15 NRSV)

That last sentence penetrated both my mind and my heart at the same time. I knew something about the Demon of Greed. We couldn't get enough of what we wanted in the days when we had more than what we needed. I thought about that as we walked home.

The gathering around the preacher in the market place was growing larger each day. Many of us who were regular attendees at these morning talks soon decided to pool our resources and we rented a store front space so that we wouldn't be distracted by the noise of the market place every day. In time other "Missionary Disciples" would visit our gathering and bring further excerpts of the words and events in the life of Jesus. Little by little all of us began to acknowledge the power of Jesus not only to cast demons out of our lives but to also transform our lives in so doing. As the demons of Greed, Hatred, Dishonesty, Cruelty, Prejudice, Racism, Jealousy, Hubris all lost their control over our daily lives we began to learn something about the power that "Change" can make in a persons life. I was beginning to sense the burgeoning and powerful sense of "change" that was happening in my life. My husband sensed it too and wanted to be a part of it and a partner in that sense of union at midlife which I felt was stronger and more loving than the words that we shared at our wedding ceremony which were frankly more ceremonial at that age than loving. My husband and I talked about that fact late into the night and we confessed that in losing everything we had in fact found everything…each other !

Now it so happened that Jesus and his apostles had taken a brief journey to Sidon for a spiritual retreat. I knew the area well. Sidon was a delightful resort on the Mediterranean Sea shore with a lovely beach known as Jonah's beach right in the center of the city. Legend has it that it was the very beach upon which the whale had spewed out Jonah onto the dry land. It wasn't long before we heard rumors from various passing caravans that Jesus and his disciples had left the city of Sidon and were returning to Galilee. Some said that he might be traveling southward on the east side of the Sea of Galilee to avoid having to pass through Samaria. Which in fact, came to be the case. Word spread rapidly throughout the area of Decapolis and in the city of Gadara. Crowds began to gather on the hillside near the city of Gadara taking along with them the lame an the halt and the blind in the hope that this Jesus, whom by now everybody had heard of, would be there to heal them. In time, as the messengers had predicted, Jesus came into view traveling with his disciples. Seeing the crowd that had gathered – which by now numbered about 4000 people – Jesus instructed them to sit down. He first healed those that had been waiting for his arrival and then he began to speak to us about the love of God that had come into the world. His presence was so transforming that it created an immediate attraction that none of us could resist. His words were so mesmerizing that we were able to immediately memorize and remember them for future study and as direction for our own lives.

My husband and I were so caught up in the moment that we stayed there on that hillside much too long. Jesus also recognized the fact that we were all tired and hungry. So he called for his disciples to get some food to feed us. They answered, as we all knew they would, that there was no store nearby. Then Jesus said, "You feed them". All together they only had seven loaves and a few small fish…but as they passed out what they had we began to realize that the bread and the fish were multiplying faster that the people could eat what was set before them. Much to everyone's surprise, when we had all eaten our fill, we still had seven baskets of food left over. In later accounts as this story was told throughout Galilee it was referred to as "The Miracle of the Feeding of the 4000". I will always remember **it as "The Miracle of No Longer Being Possessed by What I Now No Longer Possess."**

An Old Testament Text Revisited

I am writing this on my 91st birthday, there is a text in the Old Testament that has bothered me for a long time. A very long time. It is from the book of Ecclesiastes 7:8 NRSV, "Better is the end of a thing that its beginning." Now that I am coming close to the end of my life, that text is bothering me more than it did when I was younger. I discussed this concern with my physician at the time of my last physical exam, and we talked about some of the aspects of palliative care and end of life issues … all of which reminded me again of the words of Ecclesiastes which I am now beginning to disagree with more and more because my early life was such an exceptionally happy one. My brother and I attended school in Lebanon where my father was the head master. We lived across the street from our school yard where we played football, basketball and tennis ceaselessly. My memory of my childhood was that I grew up with ever-loving parents in a suburb next to the Garden of Eden. Thus it is that now, as I bear all the debilitations of aging, in a body that has fought cancer, diabetes, pernicious anemia, two strokes, and kidney failure I find it difficult to believe with Ecclesiastes that "the end of life is better than its beginning." Nowadays, I even have trouble walking from the couch to the TV to watch football, basketball and tennis. It wears me out.

Then I read a recent article in the New York Times that Earnest Hemingway once said when he write us wartime masterpiece, <u>A Farewell to Arms</u>, he rewrote the final words of that novel 39 times before he was satisfied with its ending. It occurred to me that I needed to re-examine how I intended to live out the ending of my life. I believe that I too have many more than 39 choices. One of which is to be more thankful for the loving care which family and friends have shown me, doing the little the little things in life that I used to do. Jim Spilberg, the greeter at church, readily steps up to our arriving van and opens the sliding door to get out my wheelchair, helps me get seated comfortably and before entering the church gives me a loving embrace as he opens the church door. The care that others show for me is so much greater than the casual relationships that I have known throughout my life.

Meanwhile, in order to ease my shortness of breath and the physical strain of walking I have purchased (thank you Medicare) a wheelchair that will now allow me to go to the children's soccer games and to church every Sunday. I'm beginning to feel that life couldn't be better and now have come to believe Ecclesiastes when he wrote, "the end of life is better than its beginning." I have never before received so much loving care from so many loving friends than I am receiving now, and I must admit that I am loving it!

Judas' Dilemma

(Thinking out loud)

This book of motivational vignettes has been about pulling yourself up by your bootstraps, slapping yourself on the back, self-motivation and inspiration. At least that's what I intended it to be. This concluding chapter is to forcefully remind you that there are deeper decisions in life than those I have focused on heretofore. I have spent a lifetime preaching about them and living through them as did the disciples in their day. I hope you will go beyond what I have written and encounter some of those decisions in your life. Tough decisions. Life changing decisions. Let me cite a simple example from one disciple named Judas.

Simon Peter was shocked when Jesus began to tell his disciples that it was time to prepare for him to go to Jerusalem to suffer greatly and be killed at the hands of the Scribes and the Pharisees. (Matt.16:21 NRSV). Peter responded to what he was hearing by refusing to believe what he hearing was hearing and then saying, "God forbid it, Lord. This must never happen to you." I would guess that all the disciples felt that way. That would be my response. But there was another disciple name Judas to whom Jesus had earlier promised "Separate yourself from the others and I will tell you the mysteries of the Kingdom." (Gospel of Judas pg. 111.) From that moment on Jesus constantly reassures Judas that his destiny is different from and surpasses that of all the other disciples. That day after Judas heard the disturbing news that had upset Peter, he also remembered another earlier time when Jesus had said, "If you love me you will obey my commandments." (John 14:15 NRSV) You will do what I ask of you and he felt that he had to decide time couldn't believe that a disciple (knowing the will of God) would so vociferously disagree with what Jesus was predicting. All the disciples knew and remembered the words of Jesus, "If you love me you will keep my commandments" (John 14:15) that is to say, "If you love me you will do what I tell you." Judas had to decide between believing that God had an ordained plan and Jesus was forewarning his disciples about what would soon be happening or Peter's challenging rejection of that plan. Judas who loved Jesus made the choice to heed the words of Jesus and even volunteered to be a part of God's plan. He even agreed to betray Jesus so that the plan could be fulfilled. Jesus was saying to Judas, 'the time has come for me to return to the father. Will you do me a favor?' It was a question that you would only ask of a friend ... a close friend. In acquiescing, he became what the world has since branded 'a traitor.' I feel that he was an obedient disciple who did whatever Jesus commanded or asked him to do. Jesus warned Judas that in so volunteering he would suffer many things and be reviled and condemned by the world but Judas overrode that concern with the remembrance of the words he heard Jesus say and which he could not expunge from his mind: "Greater love hath no man then this, that a man be willing to lay down his life for his friends." (John 15:13 NRSV) Understanding Christ's predestined mission, Judas chose to lay down his life for his Saviour.

Understanding the strength of the relationship between Jesus and Judas, evidenced by the intimacy of their laughter in their verbal exchanges leads me to wonder if it was to Judas that Jesus turned at the end of his life with us on this earth ... and knowing that the time had come for Him to return to the Father, he asked Judas to assist him by betraying Him in the Garden. It would, as he had earlier said, cause Judas "much grief" but who else could Jesus have asked? And Judas, because of his love and understanding and knowledge of his own destiny became a complicit participant in the death of His Lord. His betraying of Christ was a loving and enabling act of a disciple fulfilling the request of his master. Indeed, it was submitting his own desires to the providential will of God. It was Judas remembering the words of Jesus: "Greater love hath no man than this, that a man lay down is life for his friend". Such a bond was created through the laughter and friendship between Jesus and Judas. The depth and endurance of such a bond became immediately apparent to me when I turned around on the steps of Westminster Church one Sunday morning and saw old friend and colleague Max Maguire behind me and we both instantly turned each to the other, laughed uproariously and embraced.

Consequently, I no longer vilify and condemn Judas as a betrayer but I see him as one who did what his master asked him to do. I think that when Jesus nodded to Judas at the Last Supper to let him know that it was time for him to go and do what he had to do they both knew what was going to happen next which makes me wonder if the death of Judas was not suicide as recorded in Matthew 27:3-9 NRSV, but that it was accidental as recorded in the first chapter of the book of Acts 1:18 NRSV. No matter…the point is that there are greater problems in life and greater decisions to be made than those that can be resolved by the brief vignettes which I wrote and recorded for my "Today Belongs To You" TV show.

I have spent my adult life studying the problem of suicide. I even acquired a second Masters degree at Luther Seminary writing: "A Christian Approach to the Problem of Suicide". The Governor of Minnesota appointed me to a committee to study Suicide and I have articles in theological Journals on the subject. I urge you to take time each morning as you face a new day to pray to see what God has planned for you and written in your heart. (Deuteronomy 6:6 NRSV)

The dilemma of discipleship lies, as Judas discovered, in knowing that the love of Christ as well as the demands of God often makes for dilemmas in our lives.

A Bishop's Visit

My first pastorate after graduating from Princeton was a small and rather insignificant church in a small Mid-western town. Consequently, I was quite surprised one day to receive a visit from the Presbytery Executive, a personage with the demeanor and authority of a Bishop. He took me to lunch and in the course of our conversation he mentioned that he felt it was his duty to meet the new young pastors in his district and share some of his wise counsel with them. Then leaning forward across the table in the restaurant he *said in* a loud whisper, "Donald, always answer your mail." That was it? I remember grousing at the dinner table at home that evening that I was somewhat disappointed that after studying at Princeton and then Yale, my most important challenge in the parish would be to answer my mail...especially when I wasn't receiving much mail at that remote outpost.

I now realize that my Bishop was mentoring me not in terms of postal correspondence but rather he was trying to impress me with the importance of **responding to others.** To 'correspond' literally means to 'respond to another...to share yourself with another by responding to them'. That is still one of the greatest joys in life and yet we all still need to learn more about 'co-responding' to one another.

I think that is why I like the Gospels more than the epistles. In the Epistles of Paul most of his letters carry *the* tone of *sermons* or *lectures that* respond to theological questions or problems in church polity and morality rather than to issues that in many ways seem more relevant to me.

On the other hand, in the Gospels Jesus responds to all those who approached him in a personal way. Sometimes he responds with a simple touch of his hand. When Jesus saw an old woman bent over and unable to stand up straight he touched her and she immediately was healed. (Luke 13:13 NRSV) Sometime his response was simply in listening to another...as did Jesus when he encountered the Samaritan woman at the well (John 4:7-26 NRSV) Sometimes responding lies in ones ability to verbally dialogue with another... as did Jesus when he held a late evening dialogue with Nicodemus . Sometimes Jesus responded to others by entering into their lives as he did with Zacchaeus a tax collector with whom Jesus entered into conversation and then later entered into his home for dinner. So also, we see the humanity of Jesus when in hearing of the death of his friend Lazarus records that Jesus began to weep. (John 11:35 NRSV)

Likewise, I think that this is why I have gravitated to **Luther** more than I have to **Calvin** in my theological Studies...even though my diploma from Princeton is much larger and more distinctive than my diploma from Luther. Calvin was much too didactic and much too isolated from real life which becomes apparent in his _Institutes_. Whereas Luther's writings are filled with anecdotes from real life where he relates to the problems that we encounter day to day. My favorite Luther volume is entitled _Table Talk_ which is a compilation of his dinner talk conversations with over 6596 entries in the Weimar Edition. Had I kept a journal when I was younger I think I might have been somewhat close to that record number especially considering the fact that we had three women lawyers daily at our dinner table .

There is no joy greater than responding to another and thus entering into another person's life. Let me summarize it simply. I see that truth lived out daily here at home as I listen to Barb talking on the telephone to her Aunt Rosie. I hear them giggling over some silly Czech family peculiarity, or talking in a whisper so that I won't hear them, but mostly I hear them laughing with a laughter that fills our apartment with the Love they share for each other and which they share in their private 'co-responding' to words I can't hear, but with Love that I can sense.

Well, I am not a Bishop. But I am a father, and if I were having lunch with you today I think I would take a minute to emphasize the importance of co-responding with one another...even if it's just an e-mail note ...a phone call ... a touch of the hand, a look of understanding, a loving word, a sympathetic tear or maybe even just a listening ear. We all need to feel each other's uplifting Love!

Which is one reason, I suppose, that I have written this book for you.

An Overt Omission

The **Book of Psalms** begins with these words: *"Happy are they who delight in the law of the Lord, and on His law they meditate day and night."* Frankly, I've discovered that such meditation is almost always at night That's when in the moments of my insomnia the Law seeks me out to convict me of some very minor as well as some very egregious violations of God's laws in my life. And since it's my own conscience that convicts me there is no way I can escape the judgment of such condemnation. Such is the power of the conscience which consummates the dark hours of the soul until night turns into morning light

When I was in the Navy and stationed in Hawaii, I was a part of the tennis team that played in the 9th Naval District. I won the Captain's Cup two years in a row. I learned a new meaning of the word "motivation" when I realized that my tenure on the islands depended upon my continuing to win in the Navy tennis competitions. One day after a hard-fought match, a stunning young gal about my age approached me and asked if I would be interested in serving as her tennis partner in the next mixed doubles meet. In my best Jimmy Stewart mumbling style, I answered that I uh, uh, sure would. We discovered that we were well suited to be partners and soon our relationship extended on into dating … serious dating. We mostly enjoyed the soirees that the host teams provided after matches, including the dinners and dancing. One evening she mentioned to me that her father was the Commandant of Naval Base where I was stationed. She had never mentioned that before. She had previously omitted to inform me of that fact. I was stunned. I knew the Naval tradition of the separation of any amorous relationships between officers and enlisted personnel. I also realized that our relationship would ultimately end in disintegration. And it did. Slowly. I also learned that sins of omission are as equally grievous as sins of commission. An obvious fact that she had inadvertently omitted to tell me brought about the end of our relationship. Our conscience convicts us equally on both counts: sins of commission and sins of omission. Sometimes it's what you do; sometimes it's what you omit doing.

Theologically speaking, the conscience is hard to define. It's an intuitive Divine faculty that assists us in distinguishing right from wrong. Unlike the appendix, it is not something that can surgically be removed from the body. It is inherent in all of us and in all that we do. In Sunday School we read about the working of the conscience in the story of the Pharisees who had caught a woman in the act of adultery and according to the law of Moses they were ready to stone her to death at which time Jesus suggested that he who is without sin should be the one to cast the first stone. *"And they which heard it, being convicted by their own conscience, went out one by one, beginning at the eldest, even unto the last: and Jesus was left alone,* and the woman standing in the midst" (John 8:9-10 KJV) That's how the conscience works more often than not, in the middle of the night and I find myself being convicted by my conscience and wrestling with it until I'm exhausted.

When I was at Princeton studying **Calvin's** Institutes I came to understand that Calvin saw conscience as a 'Battleground' where our human will is constantly fighting the will if God. I found myself spending most of my time and energy waging war against myself in a non-productive battle with God. Then later studying in Scotland I was further ensconced in that same war with the Devil enhanced by John **Knox's** temerity to challenge the Queen with the need to further "educate her conscience ." The rule of conscience was rapidly becoming the focus of my spiritual life. A few years later I attended **Luther** Seminary in Minnesota to earn a further degree in Systematic Theology. It was for me a spiritual awakening. One day in class I heard a professor quoting Luther say: "The anguish of conscience is the beginning of faith." That sentence had the ring of truth to it I wrote it down. I spent a year studying what it meant. I came to the conclusion that the conscience was not a destructive Calvinistic battleground where I wrestled with the will of God but rather it was like Luther suggested, a profound instructive opportunity to listen to the voice of God. Insomnia became for me, not a 'Battleground' but a moment in the night when Jesus would waken me and say, "Donald, <u>we need to talk</u>" It always reminded me of my days at Princeton when I was an after class taxi-cab driver and occasionally I would see my favorite Professor, Dr. Kuist taking one of his evening walks by the campus and I would drive up to the curb and ask if I could walk with him. Then we would walk and talk and I learned more from him in those brief walks than I ever learned in his classroom. It was an interruption of my needed taxi-cab income but those walks and talks remain with me to this day as one of the most productive and memorable of my Princeton days. Likewise insomnia, when Jesus wakes me now and interrupts my needed sleep, I eagerly go and walk with Him and talk to Him and He helps me discern and understand the path I need to take.

I must stop at this point and admit that I realize that the concept of a working conscience is not a popular or readily accepted idea among a younger generation which believes in doing the expedient thing (situation ethics) rather than the right thing. It's as if they haven't studied or read about the conscience in their Bibles. And they probably haven't. The version of the Bible I used is the King James edition printed in 1612. It's been used for centuries. The RSV edition of the Bible (the version our pew racks) was printed in 1952 and it **<u>deleted</u>** the phrase: "being convicted of their own conscience." No wonder there is no understanding of a working conscience if the only mention of it in the Gospels has been deleted. (Check and compare your RSV Bible with the King James Edition) Which is why I write to you: To let an old man remind you of an old and basic truth, even though it's deleted from your modern Bible: Let your conscience be your guide, both in your sins of omission as well as your sins of commission.

A Lesson in Compassion

One of the things that I enjoyed the most on Sunday mornings at First Church in Rochester was walking into the chancel during the organ prelude and taking my seat which allowed me a full view of the gathering congregation. It was heartwarming to look out and see families coming into the sanctuary and sitting in their usual pews awaiting the start of the service. As they would walk past the chancel, it gave me a chance to nod to them, smile at them and let them know that I was glad to see them. When their children acted out, my smile always turned into a muffled laugh as I remembered those experiences in my own family life. My congregation knew that I loved them.

As I sat there in the chancel, week after week, I was constantly reminded of one of the aspects of Jesus' personality that I loved the most. Scripture records that whenever anyone approached Jesus, he always turned to them and looked upon them with compassion (love) before a conversation could start. I was learning to share those same feelings as I sat in the chancel, looking out with compassion every Sunday during the prelude before the church service began. It gave me an increasing sense of love for them. Looking out upon my congregation on Sunday mornings, I couldn't help but love them.

When Jesus encountered the widow at Nain, she was distressed and weeping as they were carrying her only son out through the city gate to his place of burial. Jesus saw her and felt compassion (love) for her and came to her because he understood her distress and sorrow. Then he walked over and touched the bier and the bearers all stood still. And he said, "young man, I say to you, 'Rise!'" The dead man sat up and began to speak. Jesus gave him to his mother. (Luke 7:13 NRSV)

The secret of compassion is to look at others and love them <u>before</u> you encounter them. Throughout scripture we read that in every encounter Jesus looked at others with compassion (love) before speaking to them. In Matthew 9:36 NRSV we read, "seeing the people, he felt compassion for them because they were distressed and dispirited." Sitting in the chancel, looking out over the congregation, I also felt compassion for them. Many were distressed and dispirited. Others were worried about many things. Still others were radiant and their smiles expressed their joy in life at that moment. Some were as Jesus said, like sheep without a shepherd. And I learned that to shepherd my flock meant to first look out among them with love.

Consequently, when the Governor appointed me to the Board of Parole in the State of Nebraska, I took with me the same sense of compassion for the prison inmates that I had for the parishioners in Rochester. When I was serving as Chairman of the Board, as every offender came through the door of the hearing room, (like parishioners coming into the sanctuary) I would look at each one of them with compassion knowing that they were distressed and dispirited. I knew they could sense my attitude toward them and that it would change the atmosphere of the meeting. Love will do that.

I knew that looking upon them with compassion might not change the results of the Board's decision to parole, but I also knew that it would change me.

An Unexpected Guest at Christmas

Christmas was always such a miraculous celebration at church. Cookies showed up daily at the church office. Meetings were by their own nature gradually transformed into yuletide celebrations. There was always the scent of candles burning and the fragrance of recently cut pine boughs decorating the chancel and lining the sills of the stained-glass windows in the sanctuary. Life at the church seemed miraculously changed. More than an annual celebration it became a constantly new encounter with the celebration of the birth of Jesus at Bethlehem.

I share all of this because I want to tell you about my Christmas at Rochester in 1985. I had lunch one day in early December at the University Club in the Kahler Hotel and happened to **encounter** a close physician friend who confided in me that a patient of his named Dr. Charles Malik, of Lebanon and former President of the United Nations Assembly was coming to Mayo's for surgery. Since I was born in Lebanon he wondered if I knew him. I said, "Know him? We went to the same school." (My Father was the Headmaster of Tripoli Boys School, a Presbyterian Mission School in Northern Lebanon.) Then I asked my friend to make arrangements for me to meet Dr. Malik's flight at the airport in order to save him the hassle of getting to his hotel…a common courtesy for many dignitaries. A few days later when his flight arrived, I was standing in the airport receiving area waiting for him to disembark. Dr. Malik is a tall man, an inch taller than I am with another inch of well coifed white hair.

You couldn't miss him…not even in a crowded airport. I walked right up to him and stood face to face in front of him while bobbing my head around him as if looking for someone. He responded in kind. Then I quietly began to whistle our old school song: "*A song of songs for the school on the hill*". Memories of his childhood flashed through his mind as he listened and looked at me. I said "Donald McCall". He blinked and then blurted out the word "Dawnie". It was an encounter of pure joy. (We had last met in 1965 when he was a guest in my Father's home at Hastings College) We embraced with tears and laughter and then I took him and his wife to their hotel and made all the arrangements necessary for their comfort and convenience during their Rochester stay.

Now, every year at Christmas time the Mayo Clinic presents a Community Wide Christmas Celebration at the Civic Auditorium. It was something like an expanded family "Evening of Caroling" with the Scriptures read and felicitations expressed. It was all "In House" and presented by the Mayo Staff. I asked the Board of Governors if this year, as an exception, they would consider asking Dr. Malik to read the Scriptures. It was always from Luke 2. They thought it was a splendid idea. He had a PhD in metaphysics from Harvard, studied Theology under Heidegger in Germany. Taught at Notre Dame, Dartmouth and other international Universities. Furthermore, Dr. Malik has received a world record of **68** Honorary Degrees (yes… **68** !) and was the past president of the United Nations General Assembly. His books on Human Rights and Christian Culture were internationally published . My favorite was entitled "*Man in The Struggle For Peace*" which I have with his autograph and resting now on that special shelf in my library.

> I picked up Dr. and Mrs. Malik on the evening of the Christmas Event and after we arrived at the City Auditorium he chose <u>not</u> to sit on the stage with the other dignitaries and presenters but rather to sit in the front row of the main floor with his wife. (I loved him for that!) When it was time for him to

read the Scriptures I helped him up to the steps of the proscenium of the stage. After placing his Bible on the lectern, he looked over the audience, scanning it as if he were looking out over the shepherd's fields of Bethlehem, then he read from Luke 2 KJV until he came to the passage "Now in <u>that country</u> there were shepherds keeping watch over their flocks by night..."

At that point he paused, took off his glasses, looked up from his Bible and said, "<u>That country</u> is <u>my country.</u>" and he began to describe the manger scene in such a personal way that we all felt that we too were encountering the birth of Jesus for the first time in our lives. You could hear a pin drop...our hearts were greatly moved ... he was investing himself in the text....and we were too. I still remember one of Dr. Malik's most memorable quotes *"**The greatest thing about any civilization is the human person, and the greatest thing about this person is the possibility of his encounter with the person of Jesus Christ.**"* The memory of those words and of that evening will be forever with me.

A few days later I was in Dr. Malik's hospital room as they were ready to take him to surgery. As we went down the hall, he reached out his hand from his gurney ... I took it in mine. It was larger than mine. After a few minutes I realized that I was not the only one at his side. Another hand... a strong hand had reached through the other side of the gurney and grasped Dr. Malik's left hand. I recognized that carpenter's hand immediately...the deep print of a large nail was still visible....I knew who **He** was...but I was too intimidated to look up into **His** face. All I remember from that encounter was that at that moment I felt a sudden sense of calm and deep peace in my life. It's that same sense of Calm and Peace which I now wish for you.

My Thankful Remembrance

When I was chairing the **Board of Parole** in Nebraska, we were preparing for an execution at the Penitentiary and someone asked me where I wanted to sit as an official observer in the execution chamber. I responded that I had no intention of observing someone else's death in the electric chair. Especially not the death of a man whom I had come to know as a friend. Furthermore, I had already witnessed one execution and it was forever ensconced in my mind. It was in a former life...years ago when I was a teenager at a church camp on the Platte River in Nebraska. Young minds are easily swayed. I had never been to a 'Sunday School' nor to a 'Church Camp' while growing up in my mostly Moslem homeland of Lebanon. Church Camp" was a totally new experience for me.

One evening at church camp as we gathered for evening devotionals we all sat around the campfire and sang an old African American Plantation Hymn, "Were You there When they Crucified My Lord?" I was strangely overcome by that experience and in my dreams that night I was transported to Golgatha on the outskirts of Jerusalem. The scene was very real to me. I was more than happy to be back in my homeland. I remember breathing through my mouth to capture the oral sweet smell of the cyclamen, the cedars and the pines. Then I noticed three crosses rising on a hill ahead of me. People had gathered around them. The man in the middle was the center of attention and I immediately recognized Him from all our church camp literature. What I saw was the Jesus whom we had been singing about that night at the campfire. The scene was so frightful that it had caused me to tremble. As I watched, I soon came to notice that others had gathered there at the foot of the cross.

Many were just people passing by. Observers who had no idea as to what they were experiencing. They were in the midst of a moment of kairos in human history and casually walked through it without seeing it. There were soldiers at the foot of the cross casting lots to divide up the few earthly possessions Jesus had owned. They were so blinded by their desire for earthly things that they had no idea of the free gift of Gods' love that was hovering above them. There were Chief Priests, Scribes and Elders who wagged their heads and threw his own words back at Him saying, "He saved others. Himself he cannot save! He trusted in God…Let God save Him!" There was a Centurian a Captain in the Roman army who supervised the crucifixion and was experienced in such matters. He was a just man and his observation was, "Surely this man is innocent". There was a Thief on a nearby cross who in repenting of his sins cried out to Jesus "Lord, remember me when you come into your kingdom". And Jesus responded, "This day thou shalt be with me in paradise". There were a few Women huddled together apart from the crowd: Mary, the mother of Jesus. Mary Magdalene. Mary the wife of Cleophas. The only Disciple there was John… the 'Beloved Disciple'.

There were others **not recorded** in Scripture. **Neither is what I saw next recorded in Holy Writ**. After Jesus had breathed his last, from the corner of my eye, I saw John the Beloved Disciple go to

Mary, the mother of Jesus who was sitting with the other women and he helped her to her feet. Then I saw John reach out his arm and place it around Mary's shoulder to comfort her on the long journey homeward. It was a loving thing to do. It was the love of heaven made known to us in this earthly life. It was the love of God made known on the cross that spilled out for us to see and understand it in human form. It was the love we were to see in Jesus and adopt as our own as we reach out to one another and put our arms around each other on our homeward journeys in this life. It's the Love that you have shared with me over the years, with your arms around my shoulders when I was your pastor that I now cherish in my memory as the love of God made known to us in this earthly life that we shared together in Rochester.

Epilogue

An Epilogue is "a piece of writing at the end of a work of literature that brings closure to the work." In this epilogue I sense that I am writing that which is not only closure at the end of this book but also closure to my own life. Now that I am 91 years of age I realize that this will probably be my last book. That fact alone makes me doubly aware of my need to express my undying thanks to many of you who have shared this life with me. To name a few:

> First, to my **Father** who from the moment of my birth embraced me in his arms and thereafter held me in his love.

> **My Children and my Stepchildren** who often didn't understand me, but who never misunderstood my love for them.

> **L. Nelson Bell,** (Billy Graham's Father in law) who would come back to my office after attending church and critique my sermons. He, like my father was an authentic Missionary.

> **William Barclay,** world renown author and preacher, who was my mentor at the University of Glasgow. His hindsight became my foresight.

John Cochran my lifetime friend.

Elaine Pagels, Princeton author and professor.

My Lebanese countryman **Charles Malik** President of the United Nations who reminded me of the land of our birth and our need to honor it.

My Psychiatrist at the Mayo Clinic (who for professional reasons remains un-named) who like a 'father confessor' helped me over the rough spots.

And

Barbara who loved me and stood by me and understood me and whom I love and will love even beyond the grave!

… and here I now lay down my pen!!

THE END

Printed in the United States
By Bookmasters